Duly and Scripturally Qualified

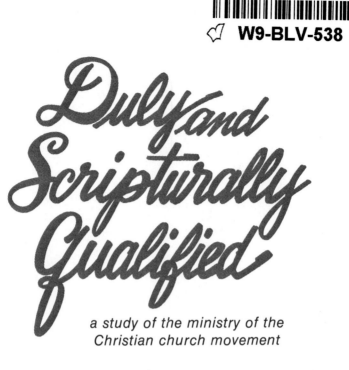

*a study of the ministry of the
Christian church movement*

by

H. EUGENE JOHNSON

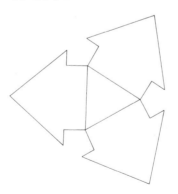

A Division of Standard Publishing
Cincinnati, Ohio
40029

ISBN: 0-87239-054-3

Library of Congress Catalog Card Number: 75-12445

Duly and Scripturally Qualified

pReface

Thomas Campbell's *Declaration and Address* of 1809 remains one of Christendom's finest pleas for Christian unity. He sought a "permanent scriptural unity." It is meaningful that the plan required allegiance from "gospel ministers" and "ministers of Jesus." Five years previous the *Last Will and Testament of the Springfield Presbytery* had willed that "candidates for the Gospel ministry" study the Scriptures and seek God's guidance in preaching the "simple Gospel."

In proposition twelve of the *Address,* Campbell addressed the challenge to "ministers duly and scripturally qualified." Wittingly or not, Campbell added a dimension—*duly.* Webster defines this as *properly* or *fitly* qualified. The history of the Campbell-Stone movement has included an unfinished chapter on the nature and qualifications of an ordered ministry.

From the beginning, advocates of this nineteenth-century reformation denounced clergymen and discussed bishops, elders, deacons, evangelists, preachers, and pastors, without developing a doctrine of the ministry. F. E. Smith recognized this:

> The basic weakness with us has been our lack of a satisfying understanding of the ministry. For the most part, we have accepted our ministry. We have loved our ministers as persons, but have not had an adequate conception of the ministry as a whole.[1]

The Campbell-Stone reformation began with an active, evangelizing, frontier interpretation of the ministry. The accent has always been on a functional ministry, as read from the written Word. Thus capable preachers, editors, and journalists have come from the midst of this people, but no one has produced a treatise on the ministry. A people who decry theology will have to find their theology in their actions and proclamations.

This volume is a survey of these actions and proclamations in some semblance of an orderly account. Students of the movement will note other areas and aspects that could have

---

[1] F. E. Smith, "Seeing We Have This Ministry," *International Convention Addresses and Reports* (1944), p. 264.

been included. Yet one of my efforts was to prune the available materials and keep a small book small.

Terminology should be clarified. "Disciples," "movement," and "brotherhood" will be used in a general historical sense. "Churches of Christ" will represent the fundamentalistic segment that formally separated from the Disciples in 1906. The "Reformers" were the Campbell group, and the "Christians," the people who followed Barton W. Stone. The body that never formally united with the Christians and Reformers, but considered Stone a founding father, was the "Christian Connexion." Since the middle of the twentieth century, another major schism has developed where the more conservative and fundamental brethren have been identified as the "Christian Churches." References to the "Disciples of Christ" since the 1950's will identify the restructured The Christian Church (Disciples of Christ), having its general offices in Indianapolis, Indiana.

The American scene dominates this study. Here the movement was born, and North America still contains more than 90 percent of the Disciples heritage.

–H. Eugene Johnson
Tampa, Florida

table of contents

1
PROLOGUE

The Frontier Spirit and Restoration Seeds

At the turn of the nineteenth century America was encompassed with a spirit of adventure. Great challenges called forth bold endeavors. It was a period of religious enthusiasm, resulting in widespread revivalism, ushering in the Second Awakening around 1790. Sixteen states were in the Union in 1800, with a population of some 5,250,000. Estimates show that only 3,000 to 3,500 churches were in the nation, and only 10 percent of the population claimed membership.

In 1790 when George Washington was inaugurated, approximately 5 percent of the population lived beyond the mountains. By 1820 some 2,600,000 people, or 27 percent of the population, were west of the high ridges.[1] The frontier increased its residents by nearly 200 percent between 1820 and 1840, while the nation as a whole gained only 80 percent. Ohio's population expanded from 50,000 in 1802 to 600,000 by 1820, becoming larger than Massachusetts.[2] In 1809 New York had 100,000 people; Buffalo and Cincinnati and St. Louis were frontier towns; and Chicago did not exist. Two days by horse were required for one to travel the 90 miles from New York City to Philadelphia.

The frontier man was individualism personified. He often read his own law, educated his children, set his own bones, built his house. He saw little need for a special priest to intervene between himself and his Maker.

The self-confident American frontier-man lacked respect for all authority, especially ecclesiastical and clerical, and his individualism led him to believe that every man had his innate ability to discover religious truth simply by a rational investigation of the Scriptures.[3]

During the early decades of the nineteenth century, the typical frontier community had several lawyers, an occasional doctor, a few Christians, and many taverns. The people were hungry for all kinds of knowledge. "In 1790 there was one newspaper in the West to 75,000 people. In 1840 there was one to 12,000 people."[4] People were eager to read and learn.

9

Several independent plantings and waterings preceded the Stone-Campbell "restoration of the ancient order." The James O'Kelly thrust began in 1792 when he withdrew from the first annual conference of the Methodist church. Going into Virginia and North Carolina, O'Kelly's group formed a separate movement. First known as Republican Methodists, in 1794 they changed their name to the Christian Church, at the suggestion of Rice Haggard. Both laity and clergy preached; the need for a bishop was denied. They proselyted heavily from the Methodists. With the opening of the Louisiana Territory in 1803, members of this Christian church traveled westward, and many were later identified with the movement of Barton W. Stone in Kentucky.

The Elias Smith-Abner Jones association was a New England reaction to Baptist Calvinism. Encouraged by the preaching of Smith, Jones formed an independent church at Lyndon, Vermont, in 1801 and called it a "Christian Church." In 1803 Smith formed a Christian church at Portsmouth, New Hampshire, and then another in Boston in 1804. This group encouraged preaching without notes to allow for the freedom of the Holy Spirit. The title "reverend" was disapproved.

A Death Wish

Barton W. Stone played the first major role in the Disciples movement. Descendant of the first Protestant governor of Maryland, Stone was born in 1772 in Port Tobacco, Maryland. When his father died just prior to the Revolutionary War, his family moved to Virginia. He received a credible academy education, and was licensed to preach in 1796. Stone waited until 1798 for ordination, partly because of Calvinistic tenets that disturbed him. He participated in the Great Awakening in 1798-1803, and was active in the famous revivals in Logan County and Cane Ridge, Kentucky.

Frustrated by the doctrine of total depravity, Stone began preaching of God's saving love—available to everyone. In 1803 he and five other Presbyterian ministers separated from the Washington Presbytery. On January 31, 1804, as the Springfield Presbytery, they produced a 144 page document, *The Apology for Renouncing the Jurisdiction of the Synod of Kentucky.*[5] Less than half a year later, on June 28, 1804, the six ministers became convinced of the unscripturalness of even their Presbytery, and dissolved it with the famous *Last Will and Testament of the Springfield Presbytery.*[6]

In the *Last Will* Stone and his associates made several references to the "preachers," "Gospel ministry," "preachers and people," and the "Reverend title" of the ministry. In the "Address" following the *Will,* the signers stated their willingness to "assist in ordaining elders, or pastors," and felt obligated to "continue in the exercises of those functions which belong to us as ministers of the gospel." Through the years Stone continued to reserve the title of "elder" for the pastor of the congregation.

The Stone movement sought "union with the Body of Christ at large" through "the law of the Spirit of life in Christ Jesus." This group grew rapidly in Kentucky, and by 1830 claimed some fifteen thousand members.

Christian Union Overture

The Stone movement was a mighty tributary, but in areas of permanent direction and force the restoration river flowed through the Campbells. The fountainhead of the Disciples' cry for Christian unity through the restoration of the principles of the New Testament church was the 1809 *Declaration and Address* penned by Thomas Campbell.

Born in County Down, Ireland, February 1, 1763; ordained to the Old Light, anti-Burgher, Seceder branch of the Presbyterian church; scholarly tutor and head of a private academy, Thomas Campbell found himself on the shores of America in 1807 seeking health and a future. In a matter of months his Presbytery, Chartiers, had lodged seven counts of formal libel against him, challenging his agapeic spirit by its procrustean bed of sectarianism.

Many historians have reported that Thomas Campbell's sense of fellowship in offering Communion to non-Presbyterians was the source of the Presbytery's anger. There is no record of such. It may be true that Campbell offered Communion to Presbyterians other than the Seceders. However, the minutes of the Presbytery do not accuse him of practicing open Communion. The second libel did refer to his objection to "holding confessions of faith before the dispensation of the Lord's Supper."[7]

Forced out of the Presbyterian ministry, alone in the New World with his family still in the British Isles, Campbell started a new ministry at age forty-six in penning the *Declaration and Address*. This fifty-six-page document became to Thomas Campbell, and his illustrious son, Alexander, who joined him in America in 1809, the foundation principles in their search for the "Christian system" and the "restoration of the New Testament church." The *Declaration and Address* was America's first treatise on ecumenicity.

In proposition twelve of the *Declaration,* Thomas Campbell listed four things necessary "to the purity of the church." The third: "that her ministers, duly and scripturally qualified, inculcate none other things than those articles of *faith and holiness* expressly revealed and enjoined in the word of God" (emphasis mine).[8] It is noteworthy that the *Declaration and Address* of fifty-six pages has fewer references to the ministry than does the two-page *Last Will and Testament.* Campbell assumed a specialized ministry. He pled for a pure and godly one.

The Campbells were adherents of the Lockean philosophy of learning—the mind being a *tabula rasa* upon which all knowledge was impressed. We learn from what we read and do. The Bible was the Word of God. However, the Campbells gave their ministries to a Christ-centered gospel. This accent upon the Christ of the Scriptures prevented them from falling off the cliff of literalistic fundamentalism.

> It was Alexander who defined faith as the acceptance of testimony, which applied to Christianity, involved not, "what do you believe?" but "in whom do you believe?" . . . it is a personal conviction regarding an unique Person as the revelation of a Personal God.[9]

Though Alexander soon took over the active leadership among the group known as the Reformers, Thomas' document and spiritual advice greatly influenced Alexander's decisions. A general discussion of the life and labors of Alexander is unnecessary here, as his basic views are widely known. His views on the ministry will be examined in a later chapter.

Voice for the Golden Oracle

In 1822, Alexander Campbell met a brilliant young man, Walter Scott, in Pittsburgh. He had received a full university education at Edinburgh, and traveled to America in 1818 when he was twenty-two years of age. He taught a year in a Long Island academy, fell victim to the lure of the wilderness, and set out walking to Pittsburgh. This "Gateway to the West" had only 1,565 residents in 1800. It was not many times larger in 1819.[10] Scott was baptized in 1820 by George Forrester, school teacher and lay preacher of a Haldane church in Pittsburgh. He assumed leadership in the academy and the church when Forrester was accidently drowned the next year. Scott's importance for the "Current Reformation" did not begin until 1827.

The Mahoning Baptist Association of Ohio, in which the Reformers had membership, had not been evangelistically successful. They reported only thirty-four baptisms from fourteen churches in 1827. Evidently the Campbellian logical, rational exposition of Scripture had more educational than motivative appeal. On Alexander Campbell's suggestion, Scott was elected as the association evangelist. This was the start of a new epoch in the reformers' movement.

Denying completely the "mourner's bench" theology, Scott saw faith unto salvation as fundamentally a rational act of accepting reliable evidence. He began preaching a "five finger" exercise: faith, repentance, baptism, remission of sins, and gift of the Holy Spirit. This was at variance with the orthodox preaching of the day.

Scott not only produced new preaching techniques, he brought to the restoration movement a new concept of Christology, based on Peter's confession in Matthew 16:16. To Scott the preaching of Christ was the preaching of the Golden Oracle. Here was precious power possible for all people. His sermonic approach found adherence among many of the brotherhood preachers, and produced excellent results.

Philosophical and Cultural Backgrounds

It would be naive to assume that the Christian church—or any religious body—arrived at any doctrinal position or expression without cultural influences. Some writers in restoration literature have implied such pristine exegesis. A wiser path requires recognition of the "non-theological factors" that have leavened the Disciples concept of preaching and preachers. Though the "big four," Thomas and Alexander Campbell, Barton W. Stone, and Walter Scott, were trained in Presbyterianism and the theology of the Westminster Confession of Faith, the Campbells and Scott reflect much of their British heritage; and Stone, the frontier spirit of a fourth-generation American.[11] This does not disregard the frontier spirit and democratic principles influencing the Campbells and Scott. The *Declaration and Address* reflects the ideology of the American constitutional experiment. Alexander and Walter came to America when only twenty-one and twenty-two years old, respectively. Both held their first public religious service in America.

It was Stone who was immersed in the American tradition. The frontier was no farther west than Pennsylvania, West Virginia, Kentucky, and Tennessee. Stone's childhood "was true frontier territory. Forests of great oaks in the Piedmont section led the people to call it the 'backwoods.' "[12] Stone was a child of the frontier revival preaching, especially that of Presbyterian James McGready. It was not McGready's lake-of-fire-and-brimstone preaching that converted the sensitive Stone, but the God-is-love message of William Hodge.[13]

Stone was eager for knowledge. Because his home community offered a lean academic diet, he enrolled in David Caldwell's "log college" near Greensboro, North Carolina, in 1790. He was eighteen years old. The school's library was sparce, but he studied Latin, Greek, and moral philosophy under the liberal Caldwell, who was a New-Light Presbyterian. Though still unlicensed, Stone taught languages in the Succoth Academy at Washington, Georgia, in 1795-1796. In Stone's background are strains of biblicism, frontier emotionalism, fascination for perfection, and struggle against ecclesiastical authority. His spirit of love and freedom pulled him out of Calvinism into Arminianism. God's love meant man's choice, not predestination.

These formative years were spent with the Bible much in

hand, head, and heart. The authority of Scripture was so compelling to Stone that when he appeared for ordination in 1798 he gave allegiance to the Westminster Confession of Faith only "as far as I see it consistent with the word of God."[14]

While in the Isles, Thomas Campell had his bouts with sectarianism and clerical isolation. He imbibed freely from the ideas of Martin Luther, John Calvin, John Wesley, John Locke, the Haldanes, John Glas, Robert Sandeman, Andrew Fuller, and Greville Ewing. Glas and Sandeman advocated these positions: faith comes not by emotion, but as a rational enterprise; the Scripturalness of a plurality of elders; weekly Lord's Supper observance; lay leadership in worship, and refusal to set certain university standards as ministerial qualifications. Alexander Campbell also was in contact with the Haldane movement through Ewing at Glasgow, and knew of their practices of congregational autonomy and believer's baptism. Alexander received much of his training in the classics, church history, and philosophy from his father.[15] John Locke was one of Alexander's favorite writers. An examination of the volumes of the *Christian Baptist* and the *Millennial Harbinger* from 1823 to 1866 discloses many articles on and by Locke, as well as evidence of a dependence upon his basic system for Scriptural interpretation. W. E. Garrison asserts that Campbell:

> read Locke's works early in life, adopted his system of philosophy, and ever afterward continued to hold it . . . we can say that he reacted against the results which it developed, but accepted in the main principles upon which it was based. His method, therefore, in so far as he had a philosophical method in his thinking, was the method of the Enlightenment.[16]

As Campbell expounded on the New Testament ministry, the influence of the Enlightenment is seen in his accent on factuality and his aversion to speculation in creedal positions. His vigorous protests against deism stem from the same line of thought. Lockean influence guided Campbell in maintaining: mankind depends upon revelation for spiritual truth; faith is related to repentance in the same manner as intellect is related to the will; and the Holy Spirit acts almost entirely through the written Word.[17]

Reid's philosophy of "Common Sense" was the dominant school of thought in Glasgow during Thomas Campbell's student days, and was not without its influence on his theology. Reid's successors were still on the faculty when Alexander enjoyed a year's study in 1808. This Scottish Common Sense approach was orthodoxy's "conservative reaction against the skepticism of Hume."[18] Realizing that Locke's position on sensationalism opened the door to skepticism, Reid asserted that the *consensus gentium,* man's common sense, constituted the "sole criterion of the validity of knowledge" and furnished the "connecting link between our subjective states and the external reality which gives value to them."[19]

These ideologies had their influences on the Campbells, but care should be taken not to force such beyond discernibility. They were indebted also to the Covenant theology of Cocceius. This Bible-centered system expounded by Professor Johannes Cocceius, a Dutch theologian of the seventeenth century, was a reaction to strict Calvinism. In the place of foreordination of individuals before birth, it accented a conception of God dealing with man in the form of two covenants—works and grace.[20] The division was placed at the fall. Interpretations encouraged by this school were deemed bold and revolutionary in the day of Cocceius. It taught that the plain and obvious meaning of Scripture was the valid one; that words in the Bible were to be taken in their normal sense and interpreted in the immediate context, without strained allegory or symbolism.

Alexander Campbell referred to Cocceius and Witsius occasionally in his periodicals. He differed little from their principles, as previously mentioned. W. E. Garrison has drawn this comparison:
1. They were intensely Biblical systems.
2. Applying ideas of successive dispensations, they held that the Old Testament was a former covenant which had passed away.
3. They reacted against a Protestant scholasticism.
4. They opposed the doctrine of predestination and sovereign, irresistible grace as tending to discourage human efforts.
5. They were practical movements, stressing conditions man must meet.[21]

Though using thought patterns from several philosophical

systems, the Campbells were slaves to none. They felt free to use elements of any philosophy that seemed to ring of truth. Their constant dream was to settle major Christian difficulties by returning to the discernible principles of the New Testament church. Because of this background, E. S. Ames has asserted that the Renaissance influenced the movement more than the Reformation.[22]

The second generation's emphasis upon the "restoration" has clouded Campbell's acknowledged dependence upon the Reformation. Campbell recognized the debt that the movement owed the Reformation. An examination of Thomas' and Alexander's early writings indicates how often they used the term "the current reformation," in giving expression of dedication to the "restoration of the first century church." They were careful students of church history. They were sharp critics of the denominational systems and "Romanism," but they were scholarly critics. In the 1849 *History of All the Religious Denominations in the United States,* Professor Robert Richardson of Bethany College, with Campbell's approval, wrote the article on the "History of the Disciples of Christ." Richardson said it was "evident" that the movement was founded upon "the two great distinguishing principles of the Lutheran Reformation": the "taking of the Bible alone as the rule of faith, to the entire exclusion of tradition; and the relying only upon that justification that is obtained through faith in Jesus Christ."[23]

In the *Christian System* Campbell acknowledged that Americans owe their "national privileges" and "civil liberties to the Protestant reformers. They achieved not only an imperishable fame for themselves, but a rich legacy for their posterity."[24] And as we compare Protestant America with Roman Catholic Spain, Portugal, and Italy, Campbell said we begin to "appreciate how much we are indebted to the intelligence, faith, and courage of Martin Luther and his heroic associates in that glorious reformation." But he adds on the same page:

> Creed and manuals, synods and councils, soon shackled the minds of men, and the spirit of reformation gradually forsook the Protestant Church, or was supplanted by the spirit of the world.[25]

The role that America played in the early foundation writings of the Disciples is weighty. Here was the promised land of theological liberty. America would give them freedom's forge to break the chains of the Old World on God's Word. William Robinson declared that Campbell "had such a veneration for democracy that he could see no 'society' acting for the church unless it was democratically representative of the Old Church."[26]

Obviously more than four men guided the formative years of the Disciples. The four were the most vocal and prolific in their expressions, but it would be error to assume that only they wrote the "textbooks" for the movement. Other early voices would include D. S. Burnet, Raccoon John Smith, Jacob Creath, Sr., Jacob Creath, Jr., John T. Johnson, John Rogers, John O'Kane, Elijah Goodwin, Robert Richardson, and Tolbert Fanning.

In an unpublished thesis, P. W. Swann described the religious origin of brotherhood ministers from 1800 to 1840.[27] He found the names of 283 preachers, but could compile biographical data on only 117. He selected sixty as a representative group. Of these, some forty-one had had some connection with the Baptist church, and fifteen with the Presbyterian. Alexander Campbell himself was closely associated with Baptist groups from 1813 (1815?) to 1830, and was considered by many contemporaries as a "reforming Baptist."

In arriving at the position of the brotherhood in the ministry we will have to consider the national backgrounds of the men, their educational attainments, their religious heritage, and the changing cultural and political climate in America. Not to be discounted is the position forced upon the Reformers in their open warfare against the established clergy. The "Kingdom of the Clergy" stood against the kingdom of God. J. J. Haley sets the scene:

> Three things had happened to bring about this ecclesiastical reign of terror: First, the Bible had been lost in the church; second, Christ had been lost in the Bible; third, the church had been lost in the world.[28]

The frontier was primed for a religious explosion. The New World would give new life to the ministry. The *Declaration and Address* believed that the "gospel ministry" could now evangelize without being under the "direct influence of the anti-christian hierarchy" or the strength and power of "the beast."[29] America hampered by neither Romanism nor Napoleon should rise to the call of God.

Notes to Chapter 1

1. James Truslow Adams, *The March of Democracy,* Vol. 11 (New York: Charles Scribner's Sons, 1933), cf. p. 110.

2. *Ibid.,* cf. p. 115.

3. David Edwin Harrell, Jr., *Quest for a Christian America* (Nashville: Disciples of Christ Historical Society, 1966), cf. pp. 28, 29.

4. R. E. Reigel, *America Moves West* (New York: Henry Hold & Co., 1930), p. 205.

5. This *Apology* is often described as a 100-page work, due to its length when reproduced in J. Rogers, *The Biography of Eld. Barton Warren Stone* (Cincinnati: American Christian Publishing Society, 1853).

6. William Garrett West, *Barton Warren Stone* (Nashville: The Disciples of Christ Historical Society, 1954), cf. pp. 76, 77.

7. William H. Hanna, *Thomas Campbell, Seceder and Christian Union Advocate* (Cincinnati: Standard Publishing, 1935), cf. pp. 33, 34.

8. *Declaration and Address* (International Convention of Disciples of Christ, 1949), p. 18.

9. Dean E. Walker, *Adventuring for Christian Unity* (printed in England, 1935), p. 24.

10. Dwight E. Stevenson, *Walter Scott: Voice of the Golden Oracle* (St. Louis: Christian Board of Publication, 1946), pp. 10-16.

11. E. E. Snoddy, "Barton W. Stone: Ambassador of the Love of God," *Voices From Cane Ridge,* edited by R. Thompson (St. Louis: Bethany Press, 1954), p. 250.

12. William West, Barton Warren Stone, p. 1.

13. *Ibid.,* cf. pp. 7-11.

14. J. Rogers, *The Biography of Eld. Barton Warren Stone* (Cincinnati: American Christian Publishing Society, 1853), p. 29.

15. W. E. Garrison, *Alexander Campbell's Theology* (St. Louis: Christian Publishing Co., 1900), contains a full treatment of Campbell's position.

16. *Ibid.,* p. 108.

17. *Ibid.* See also E. S. Ames, "The Disciples of Christ Today," *The Scroll* (October, 1935), p. 240.

18. W. E. Garrison and A. T. DeGroot, *The Disciples of Christ: A History* (St. Louis: Christian Board of Publication, 1948), p. 57.

19. W. E. Garrison, *Alexander Campbell's Theology,* p. 92.

20. V. Ferm, ed., *An Encyclopedia of Religion* (New York: Philosophical Library, Inc., 1953), cf. p. 206.

21. W. E. Garrison, *op. cit.,* cf. pp. 152, 153. See also E. S. Ames, "The Revival of Theology," *The Scroll* (March, 1935), p. 74.

22. E. S. Ames, "The Disciples of Christ: Their Great Heritage," *The Scroll* (October, 1943), cf. p. 34 ff.

23. J. Winebrenner, ed., *History of All the Religious Denominations in the United States* (Harrisburg, Pa.: Published by the editor, 1849), p. 228.

24. A. Campbell, *The Christian System* (Bethany, Forrester & Campbell, 1839), p. 3.

25. *Ibid.*

26. William Robinson, "Did Alexander Campbell Believe in Congregationalism?" *The Shane Quarterly* (January, 1954), p. 12.

27. P. W. Swann, *The Religious Origins and Educational Qualifications of the Ministers of the Christians (New Light) and the Disciples of Christ (Reformers) from 1800-1840* (Butler University, School of Religion, B.D. thesis, 1936), cf. pp. 10-15.

28. J. J. Haley, *Makers and Molders of the Reformation* (1914, reprint edition, Restoration Reprint Library, College Press), p. 19.

29. *Declaration and Address,* p. 8.

2

the priesthood of all believers

The Kingdom of the Clergy

First Peter 2:9 has remained a favorite of the movement from the beginning. The Bible was quite clear: all the members of the church were part of the "royal priesthood" under the high priesthood of Jesus Christ. *Kleros* and *laos* were both the people of God. The Campbells began their reformation with strong attacks upon the institutional clergy. Thomas believed that the power of the clergy was a major barrier to the laity's understanding of the nature of the body of Christ. Both Campbells, having suffered at the hands of the clergy, were determined to expose this hierarchical aversion of the gospel.[1] Where Thomas showed disappointment with the clergy, Alexander Campbell seemed to register anger. With the first issue of the *Christian Baptist* in 1823, Alexander identified the men of the cloth and their followers as "the kingdom of the clergy." The rulers of this kingdom had a "duty" to learn the "three grand tones: the Sabbath tone, the pulpit tone, and the praying tone."[2] These clergymen were the siblings of Pythagoras, Socrates, Plato, Aristotle, Zeno, and a myriad of pagan philosophers.[3] Campbell believed himself called of God to plumb the crooked sacerdotal wall, rip out its faulty workmanship, and prepare a new mixture of a New Testament ministry.

In 1853 Campbell was still hammering away at the "dangerous" sophism of the theorists "who rely upon their opinion of what popes, prelates and councils say." He called for another "Luther to lash the popery of false Protestants."[4] Alexander was fond of saying, "God made men, the priests made laymen." He was fond of more forceful expressions that alarmed Thomas Campbell because they ridiculed the established Protestant system. When a reader asked Alexander to prove he was "the only pious clergyman" he answered:

> I am no clergyman at all, sir, pious or impious. I once was, but I have renounced it as one of the hidden things of darkness.[5]

21

Barton Stone "agreed with Alexander Campbell's position opposing the clergy's attempt to establish or overthrow religion by law," but like Alexander's father he objected to the rough manner of snatching aside the clergy's cloaks of prestige.[6] The Protestant clergy's "pretensions to authority" put them in the same class with the "arrogant pretensions of the Papist clergy to infallibility."[7] Alexander's sarcasm was vented on the clergy who had an "eager desire" to pass themselves off as a "sort of plenipotentiaries" whose "exhortations have a peculiar efficacy in heaven and earth."[8]

Campbell was disgusted with the "intolerant zeal" of the clergy. He used the Latin phrase *Timeo Danaos ac dona ferentes*–"I fear the priests even when offering gifts."[9] However, he was much softer on Baptist preachers: "Amongst the Baptists it is to be hoped there are but few clergy; and would to God there were none." The Baptist people "had been long ago taught that the best method to keep their leaders *humble* was to keep them *poor*. And they do so."[10] Reflecting upon the position of "Father Campbell" (as Thomas Campbell was affectionately called), Robert Richardson wrote:

> There was scarcely anything in the Westminster Confession of Faith from which he felt inclined to dissent except it was the chapter which gave to the clergy a position and an authority which he thought unauthorized, and which, as he had found by experience, could be readily abused.[11]

The "sin" of silencing the people of God drew the fire of most nineteenth-century leaders. W. K. Pendleton, associate editor of the *Harbinger* and Bethany College professor, saw it more harmful than all the "withering, deadening influences that ever threw their upas shadows upon the diffusive, life-giving energy of the gospel." Nothing could be worse than locking up the "glad proclamation in the frigid forms and frozen ceremonies of a Priesthood, whether Roman or Protestant."[12]

Writings of anticlericalism are voluminous in the nineteenth century from fundamentalist and conservative leaders alike. The questions were asked: when were the apostles set aside as priests; why did Jesus say call no man Rabbi; why did the apostles continue to wear ordinary attire? The emphasis was that the primitive Christian ministry received the Spirit for service, not as an insignia of power. Benjamin Franklin was rather blunt:

> These poor little souls that desire to be like the clergy, or to be actual clergymen themselves, that want titles and the people to call them Dr., Rev., that get on the white cravat, the priestly coat buttoned up to the chin; that drop on their knees and make a pulpit private prayer as they enter the "Sacred Desk."[13]

The twentieth century has also voiced its concept of the community of the faithful as maintaining the fountain of power. E. S. Ames observed that it is "important" that the movement "maintains the essential elements of a lay movement." He agreed with Campbell as to the "real dangers in a highly specialized and professionalized clergy." Clericalism "tends to make religion appear remote from the understanding and responsibility of the common man."[14] Clarence E. Lemmon, nationally known pastor of the Disciples of Christ, gave these reasons for the anticlericalism in Disciples history:

1. This attitude was a natural reaction from the sectarian feeling of post revolutionary days.
2. Campbell's anticlericalism may have stemmed from his own psychological makeup.
3. An outgrowth from the philosophical background of the later colonial and early national period of Disciple history.
4. It has a sociological basis.
5. Reliance upon "where the Book speaks" gave a valid basis.[15]

D. Ray Lindley has expressed a position similar to Clarence Lemmon, in explaining the seeming vendetta of Alexander Campbell against the clergy, in that Campbell's crusade stemmed psychologically from "the presumption of the Presbytery of Chartiers, Washington County, Pennsylvania, in bringing charges of heresy against his father."[16] Ronald Osborn, leader of the restructured Disciples of Christ, points up the problem of the exclusive clergy.

> The sin of priestcraft has been the readiness of the sacerdotal profession to exploit the hopes and fears of the religious establishment as a base for political influence and personal comfort.[17]

Surprisingly, this minimizing of the priesthood has found support by a leading Roman Catholic theologian. Hans Kung declares:

Unlike the pagan or Jewish cult, the Christian needs no priest as mediator at the innermost part of the temple, with God himself. Rather, he is granted an ultimate immediacy to God which no ecclesiastical authority can destroy or even take away from him.[18]

Within the past twenty years the Disciples of Christ have experienced a strong surge for a separated professional ministry. The words "clergy" and "clergyman" have appeared with increasing frequency and approbation in Disciples of Christ periodicals and official pronouncements. In ecumenical meetings and social action groups, Disciples of Christ ministers are occasionally seen attired in clerical collars. A considerable number now wear clerical robes and vestments while in the pulpit. Perhaps E. S. Ames would see "danger" signs in these symbols of a "professionalized clergy."

Ministerial Titles

The Disciples of Christ professional ministry appears to have advanced beyond the appreciation of their general membership in comfortable usage of the terms "reverend" and "clergyman." It would be uncommon for a layman of the Restructured Disciples to designate his pastor as a clergyman. However, a study of "Letters to the Editors" of Disciples of Christ periodicals in the last several years rarely reveals any objection to the clerical designations used by individual ministers and the regional and national components of the church.

Alexander Campbell felt as compelled to attack clerical titles as he did the clerics. He liked to compare the titles given clergymen with the abundance of honorary titles of a military nature. He marveled at the Doctors of Divinity who did no doctoring. "Never was there a church militant so rich in honorary distinctions, with so few real Christians, as the church militant of America."[19] Beginning with the August, 1826, issue of the *Christian Baptist* Campbell carried Matthew 23:8-10 on the masthead. Both Thomas and Alexander Campbell believed that the Scriptures reserved the title "reverend" for God only. To designate himself as a minister, for many years Thomas would occasionally annex to his name the initials V.D.M.—*Verbi Divini Minister,* "Minister of the Word of God."

Perhaps in jest or spiritual sarcasm Alexander, in his pre-*Christian Baptist* period, would add to his name the initials V.D.S.—*Verbi Divini Servus,* "Servant of the Word of God." It proved a telling contrast to the "D.D.'s" so generously used by his contemporaries.[20]

In 1853 a reader inquired of the *Harbinger* if an evangelist could assume the honorary title of reverend. The terse reply of a co-editor listed many titles from "Reverend" to "Lord God the Pope" and concluded: these are all "titles of the same category, and we have placed them in the ascending series, from the positive of spiritual pride to the superlative of blasphemy."[21]

Many view Isaac Errett as the successor to the mantle of Alexander Campbell. However, in 1863 when he received from his congregation a gift of a doorplate with "Rev." on it, he discovered quickly the resentment of the brotherhood leaders. Thomas Munnell, writing for the scholarly journal, *The Christian Quarterly,* had this to say of ministerial prestige:

> Would you study medicine awhile for the name *Doctor?*–a cheap counterfeit of D.D.? Rabbi used to be no insignificant title, though a little under par with the Savior.

He looked over the list of clerical titles and concluded that "only small men feel the need of such aid to give them consequence in the world."[22]

In 1906 the editor of the conservative *Christian Standard* was disturbed over the practices of certain administrators addressing mail to local ministers including "Rev." He wrote: "There is neither sense nor religion in missionary secretaries addressing their preaching brethren by the title of 'Reverend.' " He called it a "needless offense."[23] A 1951 article demanded why any man would wish to "appropriate this title 'Reverend,' which the Scriptures give to God alone." Was it not an "implicit attempt to 'be as gods,' silently suggested by Satan?"[24] This aversion is still an emphasis with the *Standard* and the more conservative *Restoration Herald* and *Gospel Advocate.* A survey of the *Advocate* for the past several years indicates a preference for the designation "preacher." In fact, the churches of Christ have shown little change in their opposition to ministerial titles in the last seventy-five years. There has been one ironic change among the Christian church group in this same period of time. A survey of periodicals, literature, and advertisement shows a fondness for the title Doctor of Divinity among the "reverend haters."

The Common Ministry

T. W. Manson, the British scholar, describes Christian service as "not a stepping stone to nobility, it is nobility." The Disciples movement began with the dream of a serving church. Service—ministry—"is both a gift from Christ to his church and a command defining the task of the church."[25] Without demeaning "public preachers," Alexander Campbell asserted that "all Christians are preachers, in some department of society, and that if ever this is lost sight of, there is an end of reformation."[26] The people of God were classless. Campbell's denunciation of the clergy was as a class, not as an order. He did exercise Christian benevolence toward them as men. A priest had no more right to divide the unity of the church than did a king to rule subjects. It was the "glory of Christians to be men in Christ—to be free men too."[27] In the Christian System Campbell expressed the equality of all citizens in Christ's kingdom, "equal rights, privileges and immunities." Therefore, a Christian "may of right preach, baptize, and dispense the supper, as well as pray for all men, when circumstances demand it."[28]

Benjamin Franklin, fundamentalist leader and "publication rival" of Isaac Errett, asserted in 1859 that the movement could boast of three thousand preachers. W. K. Pendleton replied in the spirit of evangelism: "I trust we have more. In one sense, we should have three hundred thousand—one in every disciple."[29]

Accurate statistics are difficult for the years up to 1860, but it is conservatively estimated that the Brotherhood grew, largely by lay evangelism, from twenty thousand at the 1832 merger of the Reformers and Christians to some 250,000 in 1860. This is a fantastic increase without benefit of immigration, but with a certain success in proselyting.

In the nineteenth century in America the accent for the "priesthood of all believers" often appeared to be a polemic against the clergy. British expressions were usually more positive. David King noted:

There is, then, no clerical caste, or order, in the Church of God— all the laity of God are the clergy of God, . . . taking the term "Reverend" as applied to the clergy of our time, we have of course, to deal with it in its common signification, and then it stands as "venerable"—"one worthy of *reverence.*" It is not wrong to designate a person venerable who really is so; but it cannot be improper to apply the term *reverend* to any worthy Christian (man or woman) whose character really corresponds. But the use of the term to designate the "clergy" as distinguished from the *"laity"* is of the Apostasy; both *un*scriptural and *anti*scriptural.[30]

King sought a "return to ministry" as authorized by Jesus. Thus each Christian could "become an evangelist and set the church in order." A more positive approach finds expression today. Paul Benjamin, Bible-college professor, declares:

If a congregation takes the New Testament idea of ministry seriously, one can no longer speak of a congregation and the minister, but rather of a ministering-congregation.[31]

With the growing development of a public ministry and its specialization, the Disciples movement, in all its phases, has grown slower numerically in the twentieth century, though churches of Christ appear to have slowed the least. Particularly the Disciples of Christ for more than a decade have shown a percentage increase less than the general population increase in the United States.

The 1970-1971 *Year Book of Christian Churches (Disciples of Christ)* contains a chart "World Membership Since 1879." The number of churches for 1970 is 7,097, the lowest number (excluding 1969 of 7,019) since 1897. Yet the total number of ministers, 8,518, is the greatest since 1897, excluding the three years of 1958, 1968, and 1969. Again, the total world membership of the Disciples of Christ of 1,735,820 for 1970 is the lowest since 1933. The Disciples of Christ membership grew only half as fast as the general population during 1940-1950, as reported in a 1955 UCMS pamphlet "Facts About Our Churches and a Changing America." There appears to be a relationship between a vigorous and aggressive ordered ministry and the effectiveness of the mutual ministry of the saints of God.

The "Pension Fund Bulletin" (May, 1967) carried the report that the Disciples of Christ "ordained 87 persons to the Christian ministry during 1966. This is 20 less than 1965, when 107 were ordained, and 25 less than 1964, when 112 were ordained." A shortage of pastors is evident in this segment even though there is no appreciable shortage of ministers.

The untapped potential of the laity has been termed "God's frozen people." The "mutual ministry of the people" for many decades has been largely confined to expressions of public worship. The current emphasis is for a "ministry in life" to the church and to society.[32] On the frontier every Disciple was a faith fighter. He (she) carried his New Testament with him daily and fed its thoughts to anyone who appeared hungry. At times it was forced feeding. How far some elements of the tradition have drifted in emphasis can be gleaned from a 1972 article in the *Christian,* decrying the decline of pastoral visitation:

> "A *new day* is dawning in the Body of Christ; a *new Church* is emerging. In it the laity is discovering the nature of ministry as a task common to their calling, as well as that of the *clergyman"* (emphasis mine).[33]

Canon Douglas Webster stated:

> The idea of priesthood is found in a number of religions in one form or another, but the idea of ministry is unique in Christianity. In Hinduism and Buddhism there are priests and monks. There are imans and mulas in Islam. There were the priests and now the rabbis in Judaism. . . . These classes were not concerned with any wider form of service or ministry in the Christian sense of that word. On the other hand, at the heart of the Christian Gospel, there is this whole idea of ministry.[34]

The Disciples' tradition has continued to affirm the New Testament position that ministry is a spiritual function more than an office.

Administering the Ordinances

Taking their cue from the early advocates of the Way—Paul, tentmaker; Peter, fisherman—the Reformers advocated the non-professional adminisration of the church ordinances.[35] Of the prerogatives of the ministry, Barton Stone retained more of his denominational training than did the Campbells. The Christians maintained that only an ordained minister could officiate at the Lord's Supper. The failure to observe the Supper in the absence of a minister is noted in Stone's advice: "Should you have no preacher meet and read the scriptures, sing, pray and exhort one another. Let a part of the day be devoted to the instruction of our children in the scripture."[36] James DeForest Murch gives an interesting correlation in his 1937 *Christian Minister's Manual:* "The chairman of the elders should appoint two elders a month (or each Lord's Day) to preside at the Table. The *minister will attend at all times"* (emphasis mine).[37]

This difference resulted in a three year delay of union between a Reformer and a Christian congregation in Lexington, Kentucky, around 1835.[38] Of this delay of union in Lexington, Campbell attacked the position of the Christians:

> They could not think of the *weekly* meeting for Christian worship, nor of receiving the emblems and memorials of the great sacrifice, unless consecrated and presented by the hands of one ordained by men to minister at the altar, . . . The New Testament, indeed, could not be a bond of union to those thus traditionized; for it knows no such usages.[39]

Isaac Errett felt largely as did Campbell concerning the Supper. "There is positively nothing in the New Testament making it necessary that this should be presided over by an ordained minister; all Christians are priests to God."[40] Campbell asserted on many occasions that his concepts of believers' priesthood, the identity of the "clergy" and "laity" never varied through the years. D. Ray Lindley detects a change:

> Thus the three stages of Campbell's thought regarding the priesthood of believers performing the functions of the ministry were: in the beginning he believed they were under a scriptural injunction to perform them, since they were all "preachers of the word"; later he held that they were permitted to perform them in the absence of regularly ordained officers; finally he insisted they were unauthorized to perform them without the consent of the Christian Community.[41]

It is customary today in all segments of the movement for elders and deacons to conduct the service of the Supper, without the participation of the preacher or minister. When the minister does participate it is in the role of a meditator or in handing the loaf and cup to the elders prior to their prayers.

In an increasing number of Christian churches and Disciples of Christ congregations the minister visibly breaks a loaf of bread before the congregation, even though broken wafers or individual pieces are distributed to the congregation. G. Edwin Osborn, of the Graduate Seminary at Phillips University, believed the essence of the ordinance was expressed as each "receives the bread and breaks it (performing his own 'fraction' as his priest in the sight of God)" and then receives "his individual cup from the tray" rather than from the "hand of an administering priest."[42]

Today rarely does a member of a congregation perform the ordinance of baptism. In the churches of Christ it is administered by the evangelist or an elder. In the Christian churches and the Disciples of Christ the preacher or pastor performs the rite. This has been the result of many influences: the developing philosophy of the specialized ministry; baptism's nature as once-for-all initiation into the fellowship; and perhaps the practice and skill necessary for a "pleasing performance."

Notes to Chapter 2

1. (a) W. E. Garrison and A. T. DeGroot, *The Disciples of Christ: A History* (St. Louis: Christian Board of Publication, 1948), p. 341.

(b) W. T. Moore, *The Plea of the Disciples of Christ* (Chicago: Christian Century Co., 1906), p. 48.

(c) See the *Millennial Harbinger* (April, 1834), p. 148, for A. Campbell's view on clergy who "keep up divisions."

2. A. Campbell, *Christian Baptist* (Buffalo: Brook County, Virginia: January, (1824), p. 101.

3. *Ibid.,* (April, 1824) cf. p. 156.

4. *Millennial Harbinger* (February, 1853), p. 63.

5. *Christian Baptist* (January, 1824, Vol. I, reprint, Gospel Advocate Company), p. 109.

6. West, *op. cit.,* p. 135.

7. *Christian Baptist,* Vol. II (August, 1824), p. 248.

8. *Ibid.,* p. 3.

9. *Christian Baptist,* Vol. VII (June, 1830) reprint, pp. 279, 280.

10. *Ibid.,* p. 45. cf. *Christian Baptist,* Vol. VII (May, 1830), p. 235 for a similar view.

11. Robert Richardson, *Memoirs of Alexander Campbell* (Standard Publishing, 1869 reprint), Vol. I., p. 232.

12. W. K. Pendleton, "Every Christian a Preacher," *Millennial Harbinger* (April, 1854), p. 215.

13. Otis L. Castleberry, *They Heard Him Gladly* (Old Paths Publishing Co., 1963), p. 63.

14. E. S. Ames, "Disciples Appraise Themselves," *The Scroll* (April, 1942), p. 333.

15. Clarence E. Lemmon, "An Evaluation of Our Ministry," *The Reformation of Tradition,* Ronald E. Osborn, ed. (St. Louis: Bethany Press, 1963), cf. pp. 202-205.

16. D. Ray Lindley, *Apostle of Freedom* (St. Louis: Bethany Press, 1957), p. 15.

17. Ronald E. Osborn, *In Christ's Place: Christian Ministry in Today's World* (St. Louis: Bethany Press, 1967), p. 116.

18. Hans Kung, *Why Priests?* (New York: Doubleday and Co., 1972), p. 28.

19. *Millennial Harbinger* (September, 1830), p. 427.

20. Robert Richardson, *Memoirs of Alexander Campbell,* 1868 (Standard Publishing, reprint), Vol. I, p. 335.

21. *Millennial Harbinger* (August, 1853), p. 473.

22. T. Munnell, "Indolent Preachers," *The Christian Quarterly* (January, 1871), p. 107.

23. James A. Lord, *Christian Standard* (February 10, 1906), p. 216.

24. R. D. Scott, *Christian Standard* (June 9, 1951), p. 364.

25. W. B. Blakemore, "The Christian's Task and the Church's Ministry," *The Revival of the Churches,* Vol. III (St. Louis: Bethany Press, 1963), p. 153.

26. *Millennial Harbinger* (1832), p. 249.

27. *Christian Baptist,* Vol. I, reprint, p. 94.

28. *The Christian System,* (reprint), p. 64.

29. *Millennial Harbinger* (December, 1859), p. 710.

30. Louise King, *Memoirs of David King,* 1895?; (College Press: Restoration Reprint Library, reprint), pp. 252, 253.

31. Paul Benjamin, *The Growing Congregation* (Lincoln Christian College Press, 1972), p. 31.

32. cf. Keith R. Bowes, "Our Contemporary Contribution," *The European Evangelist* (June, 1971).

33. Stephen J. Brock, "Pastoral Calling Revisited," *The Christian* (April 23, 1972), p. 9.

34. Canon Douglas Webster, "The New Testament Concept of the Ministry," Lecture at Selby Oak College, April 24-25, 1969, Birmingham, England.

35. The word "sacrament" traditionally has been shunned by the movement. The British scholar William Robinson felt it had been unwisely denied a rightful place. See H. E. Short, *Doctrine and Thought of the Disciples of Christ* (St. Louis: Christian Board of Publication, 1953), p. 33. Since the mid-century usage of "sacrament" has increased in Disciples of Christ writings.

36. B. W. Stone, "An Address to the Elders, Preachers and Brethren in the Church of Christ," *Christian Messenger,* Vol. II, (January, 1828), p. 63.

37. J. D. Murch, *Christian Ministers Manual* (Cincinnati: Standard Publishing, 1937), p. 63.

38. West, *Barton Warren Stone,* p. 172.

39. *Millennial Harbinger* (1832), p. 194.

40. Isaac Errett, *The Querists' Drawer* (Cincinnati: Standard Publishing, 1910), p. 264.

41. D. Ray Lindley, *Apostle of Freedom* (St. Louis: Bethany Press, 1957), p. 115.

42. Personal letter from Dr. G. E. Osborn, September 6, 1954.

the threefold ministry

The Ministry in the Laity

The nature of the ministry advocated by the early leadership of the Disciples has been misunderstood often in this century. A typical misconstruing is seen in the 1954 article James E. Craig wrote for *Look* magazine. He jumped from the pronouncement "Disciples do not accept the doctrine of Apostolic succession" to the non sequitur: "They interpret the New Testament words for 'bishop' and 'elder' as synonymous for a single *lay office*" (emphasis mine).[1] This was reinforced by: "no important distinction was made between clergy and laity. Indeed, any elder could perform any *ministerial* duty—except that of marriage ceremonies" (emphasis mine). Many have misunderstood the role of congregational leadership because it was non-clergy and often non-salaried. Even W. E. Garrison referred to the eldership as "lay officers."[2]

Greater clarity is seen concerning the Campbell-Stone position in the 1947 British *Report of the Commission on the Ministry:* "There is a clear distinction in the New Testament between the ordained ministry and the unordained members of the Church."[3] W. B. Blakemore, dean of the Disciples Divinity House at Chicago, in an ordination charge, denied the assertion that Disciples "make no distinction between clergy and laity." To him such a belief "contradicts our deepest tradition," and "belies our historic and continuing practice." Our ministers do have special powers, but "no powers other than those given to it by the laity."[4] More than a decade later Blakemore admonished:

> To reduce the elder virtually to a lay officer among other lay officers is to miss the whole point of the eldership as it has existed since apostolic times—namely, as sharing the burden of spiritual leadership of the congregation.[5]

Unfortunately, the role of the eldership has suffered reduction in the Disciples of Christ, particularly in the last quarter century as the agency leadership endorsed the "functional church pattern." This approach accented work divisions within the congregation chaired by appointed leadership. This emphasis has reduced the "spiritual leadership" of the eldership to public worship functions and visitation to the sick. In the 1960's, the United Christian Missionary Society (UCMS) published a booklet, *You Are an Elder,* by W. H. Knight. It commences in explaining that since the "elder was once given such a broad responsibility" he failed to do an adequate job, the situation being remedied by organizing in "a departmental, functional pattern." For example the Department of Worship in public worship would control the "elders, deacons, deaconesses and ushers." This ten-page pamphlet has no reference to the use or study of the Scriptures. Duties of the elders include "serve at the Lord's Table" and "cooperate with the functional departments." Yet there is no reason that a functional pattern cannot be used effectively under the control of the eldership as historically evaluated.

In a polite debate with James Shannon in the *Harbinger* in 1839, Thomas Campbell felt Shannon's position so stressed the priesthood of believers that it slighted the ministry. "And if all the disciples be bound by a moral necessity to preach and baptize, why all the special directions given to Timothy and Titus about choosing and ordaining fit persons for teaching and ruling in the churches?"[6] Father Campbell saw no conflict between a universal "priesthood" and a set-apart ministry. In 1832 when taken to task for the supposed irresponsible leadership among the Reformers, Alexander Campbell admitted they taught that any Christian who "finds an unbeliever, has a right and command *to preach* to him the gospel, and to baptize him if he asks it of him." Yet:

> We have no idea that every disciple is to become a public preacher, baptizer, teacher, critic, commentator, at his own volition, option, or solicitation, by virtue of his discipleship, or to act in any public capacity in any society, . . . except by special designation and appointment of the community or communities in which or for which he acts.[7]

In the *Christian System,* in the chapter on "The Christian Ministry," Campbell states that the "extraordinary gifts" to the apostles and prophets terminated when the church was "fully developed and established." He concluded: "The standing and immutable ministry of the Christian community is composed of Bishops, Deacons, and Evangelists."[8] In 1849 Campbell was saying that the ordinance and support of the ministry "is as positive and as clear from the New Testament, as the institution of baptism, the Lord's day and the Lord's supper."[9] Isaac Errett defended the distinction between the ministry and the brotherhood by stating it was "for the sake of *order* and *efficiency,* in accomplishing the purposes of the commission" that a *"division of labor* takes place among the partners in this most holy enterprise."[10]

In the *Christian System,* Campbell described the threefold ministry of the primitive church. *Bishops* were to "preside over, to instruct, and to edify the community." *Deacons* were "servants—whether called treasurers, almoners, stewards, door keepers, or messengers." *Evangelists,* though a class of "public functionaries created by the church, do not serve it directly;" they were "devoted to the preaching of the word, to the making of converts, and the planting of churches."[11] The great majority of Reformers did not follow Campbell's lead in using the term "bishop." The practice was to give the "spiritual leader" of the congregation the title of "elder." It is of interest that at the beginning of the second century, the *Didache* (the complete title of which is translated *The Teaching of the Lord Through the Twelve Apostles to the Gentiles)* gave prominence to the *bishopric* as a multiple congregational office. "Elect therefore for yourselves bishops and deacons worthy of the Lord, men that are gentle and not covetous, true men and approved" (Chapter XV).[12]

A. The Eldership

From the very beginning of the "Current Reformation" the leadership made exhaustive studies to show the parallelism in the office of *presbuteros* (elder), *episkopos* (bishop) and *poimain* (pastor).[13] *Bishop* implied no area control of churches or ecclesiastical rank above the preacher. F. M. Green stated in his *Manual:*

> It is quite generally conceded that in the church of Christ, the term bishop, elder or overseer, and pastor refer to the various elements which are found in the same ecclesiastical office. In the first is the executive idea of presidency, in the second of oversight, moderation and experience; and in the third that of feeding or tending as a shepherd the flock of God.[14]

There is, however, a contrary note, by an anonymous writer, in the January, 1872, issue of *The Christian Quarterly*. He boldly asserted that the "one grand cardinal feature" of the apostolic church was its "episcopal" form of government. He proclaimed:

> The churches came forth into history, each led by its bishop, like a flock. There is no exception anywhere. . . . There is no suspicion or hint of congregationalism. . . . In subordination to the bishop, the elders and the deacons watch over, rule over, teach, and feed the flock. They constitute his council.[15]

More reason to remain unknown is found when the writer concluded that "the study of the primitive Church is a study of embryology." Thus there is no blueprint in the New Testament, "only tendencies, forces, forms which God is quickening into life, but which are yet all imperfect."[16] W. W. Wasson suggests this might be from the pen of the "great liberal" L. L. Pinkerton. This is substantially the view of the British *Report* of 1947: "From the first half of the second century, the separate ministries of Bishop, Presbyter, and Deacon gradually became universal." It is quite feasible that the "presiding elder" or the "pastor elder" of the first century became the sole bishop of the congregation in the second century.

Other than Alexander Campbell, most preachers preferred the title "elder." William Baxter used the title for his biography, *Life of Elder Walter Scott;* J. A. Williams did likewise in his *Life of Elder John Smith.* In the "Preface" written in 1870 Williams gave recognition to those who helped him "in collecting material" and mentioned such as Absolom Rice, James Challen, Robert Richardson, Philip S. Fall, Aylett Raines, John Rogers, L. L. Pinkerton, and Isaac Errett— identifying them all with the designation of "Elder." Though many of the pioneer preachers were itinerate, or traveled a preaching circuit establishing churches, rarely did they use the designation of *Evangelist* before the 1870's.

> Until well toward the end of the nineteenth century, and perhaps later in some places, it was customary for a minister who was entering upon a new pastorate to respond to the "invitation" at the end of his first sermon, take his place on the front pew, and be received into the membership of the church by one of the elders, after which a meeting of the congregation was called and the new pastor was elected as an elder.[17]

Alexander Campbell was "regularly ordained one of the Elders of the Church of Christ at Brush Run."[18]

In 1862 Madison Evans produced sketches of twenty-four pioneer preachers. All were identified as "elder" except John Longley, who was called "Father Longley," having been born in 1782.[19] In the obituary of Longley's wife in the October, 1826, *Christian Messenger* he was identified as "Elder John Longley."

The influence of Alexander Campbell is shown in the refusal of the frontier churches to give their ministers any status "superior to the general eldership. He was considered to be an elder rendering certain special services essential to the well being of the congregation."[20] When Barton Stone described Nance, Read, and Rice Haggard uniting with his movement he called them "three valuable elders." Stone seemed to reserve "elder" for the local, ordained minister in the Christian Connexion.

Campbell performed more as an evangelist than a congregation's elder in much of his ministry. He toured, debated, held "protracted meetings," influenced the movement as editor and author. He assumed the role of an evangelist when he journeyed to Nashville, and from the pulpit of the church denounced its minister, J. B. Ferguson, for three consecutive nights. He returned to Bethany and carried his victory into print under "The Fall of Mr. J. B. Ferguson."[21] Richardson said Jesse Ferguson became involved in "spiritualism" and "post-mortem gospel."[22] Campbell's conduct seems at odds with his prior pronouncement in the *Christian Baptist:*

> Call not bitter sweet, nor sweet bitter. Let us not call the messenger of a congregation, an elder. Let us not call a preacher, a bishop. Let us not call a bishop, a divine, nor a deacon, a ruling elder. In a word, let us give to divine institutions divine names, and to human institutions human names.

and

> If they are *sent* to preach, let them go to preach—*but they can plead no right to officiate as bishops under the call to preach.*[23]

Campbell saw an immutable ministry in the primitive church—three and only three classes of ministers. The "pastors" and "teachers" of Ephesians 4:11-13 were easily explained:

It is evident that these apostles, prophets, evangelists, pastors and teachers, were all *supernatural* characters, for a precise object ("fitting the saints for the work of the ministry") and for a limited time; that this object was answered by their discourses and writings, and, that this limited time has expired.[24]

Thus these pastors and teachers must "be distinguished from the ordinary bishops or elders of a Christian church."[25]

Ronald Osborn has observed the changing concept of the eldership, particularly in the restructured Disciples of Christ.

The nineteenth century eldership was the ministry of Word, sacrament, and pastoral oversight. The emergence of the "one-man pastoral system" with salaried ministers, now ordained only after meeting educational requirements in a theological seminary, and the concurrent diminution of the eldership in importance have served to obscure its earlier character.[26]

The Necessity of a Wife

There was general assent in the nineteenth-century movement that the eldership was the highest spiritual office in the church. The qualifications in 1 Timothy 3:1-7 and Titus 1:5-9 played an important part in all discussions and debates. Campbell believed that these passages required an elder to be married. "A man who has had no experience in domestic management is illy qualified to manage the family of God."[27] The scholarly J. W. McGarvey in his *A Treatise on the Eldership* held the same, concerning 1 Timothy 3:2, *mias gunaikos andra* (married only once). He reasoned:

We think that candor requires the admission that it also has the effect of requiring a man to be a married man. That he should be the husband of one wife, forbids having less than one as clearly as it forbids having more than one.[28]

McGarvey was not impressed with the argument that his interpretation would disqualify Paul, Barnabas, and Timothy from the eldership. However, using his logic with "having his children in subjection" would require that a married elder have children. McGarvey nimbly avoided this issue.[29]

Robert Milligan differed with Campbell on this issue of a married elder with children. He could not accept any logic that excluded celibacy. "It is not probable that Paul would condemn in all others what he considered right in his own case. It is unreasonable to suppose that the chief of all the Apostles would lay down as a necessary qualification for inferior officers what is proved, by his own example, to be unnecessary for the superior."[30] W. R. Walker seems to have spoken for the majority of the Christian church segment in the middle twentieth century on this point. He reasoned similarly with Milligan. "In his letters to Timothy and Titus Paul lists the qualifications for *ideal elders and deacons.* How many such can be found? None but a dictatorial egotist would dare accept office in the local church if all mentioned virtues were insisted upon."[31] This view has been continued by a feature writer of *The Lookout,* Noble Tribble. He could not accept a narrow view of 1 Timothy 3:2. "There are other considerations which lead me to believe that celibacy does not disqualify a man for the office of elder or deacon." He quotes Richardson and adds: "Children are not a qualification; but the way children are reared is."[32]

Churches of Christ Outlook

The churches of Christ have largely remained Campbellian in their concept of the eldership. The eldership controls all matters of the church, being assisted by the other ministerial offices. Daniel Sommer, a leader of the non-instrumental brethren, stated in 1910 a position respected today.

> The Church is a monarchy: Jesus Christ is King, the New Testament is his statute book, the overseers (otherwise spoken of as elders, or bishops) with deacons and evangelists, are the chief executors of the divine will in the Church.[33]

H. Leo Boles agreed in his volume on the *Eldership,* being convinced that "All of the authority that Christ has left upon earth for the government of his people has been vested in the elders."[34]

The preacher in the churches of Christ occupies a much less authoritative position than his counterpart in the Disciples of Christ and the Christian churches. Boles explained, "We use the word 'preacher' for the New Testament word 'Evangelist'. . . The evangelist was the one who preached the glad tidings and had no reference whatever to any official class." Boles emphatically declared "The work of an evangelist is under the eldership of the church." The spiritual power of the eldership is such that "For a preacher to rebel against the Scriptural eldership of the church is to rebel against God and his order of organization."[35]

We will not assume that the leading writers and ministers of a segment of the movement represent more than a major position. The F. L. Colley-W. C. Ketcherside debate in Dallas in 1954 over the proposition of the Scripturalness of elders securing a preacher as a minister attests to the diversity in the churches of Christ. Ketcherside took the position that as long as "a congregation is properly organized and functioning with a faithful eldership, there is no work which an evangelist has as an integral part of that congregation."[36] Again, Ketcherside's position is reminiscent of Campbell's address before the Kentucky Convention of Churches in 1853, where he spoke strongly against the custom of some churches "of depending too much upon itinerant preachers, and neglecting to call forth and employ the gifts of their own members in mutual exhortation and instruction." Richardson reported that Alexander "dwelt much upon the importance of a proper eldership to teach and exhort from house to house."[37]

The Abilene Christian College (Bible) Lectures have been a focal point of leading thought among the non-musical instrument churches. Through the years, the expressions are consistent on the role and authority of the eldership. In the 1921-1922 *Lectures,* O. H. Colley cautioned preachers who "try to be both elders and preachers." He concluded, "The elders were to rule (1 Timothy 5:17). They were to take the oversight of the church (1 Peter 5:1)."[38] That same year W. G. Malcomson added:

> The elders of the church are responsible for judging and ruling as to the character and extent of its ministers and public ministrations.[39]

In the 1946 *Lectures* J. H. Richards proposed the same line of authority in advising the elders that they "should feel a responsibility in counseling with the evangelist" upon any subject matter "when they see the need for it."[40]

Basic Differences

There appear to be basic differences in the overall position and authority of the eldership in the Christian churches,

churches of Christ, and Disciples of Christ in at least three areas: one, what constitutes the *esse* of the congregation; two, the area of control; three, the length of service. The Christian churches generally hold the position of the British preacher, David King, that "a church without a plurality of elders . . . has not attained the *full stature* of the church of the New Testament."[41] Therefore elders "are not essential to the *being* but to the *well-being* of a church."[42] This is the position taken by J. W. McGarvey in his *Treatise on the Eldership:*

> We freely admit that churches are found at the present day without a plurality of members qualified for the Eldership; and some, perhaps, without even a single member thus qualified. And even admit that such churches need not have a plurality of Elders or any Elders at all. Indeed, they *must* have none until they can have more than one who is qualified.[43]

Leo Boles states the opposition:

> A church is a church only when it is fully organized. It cannot be properly termed a "church" in its completeness until it has all of the essential qualities of a New Testament church.[44]

On the point of control, the non-instrumental group sees the eldership in total control. An editorial in the *Gospel Advocate* states the fallacy of some who believe the elders "have the oversight of the *spiritual* side of the work of the church and the deacons have oversight of the material side of the work of the church. For this sentiment there is not a vestige of authority in the New Testament."[45] The Disciples of Christ outlook is summarized by Chester A. Sellars in his weekly column "A Chat with Chet," in reply to a question about "the governing body" of the congregation. "That word 'rule' is disconcerting. The elders and deacons have specific duties to perform. These do not include 'ruling.' They serve the congregation."[46] David Lipscomb put it quite differently:

> The church can give the elders no authority. The church is not the source of authority for elders or other Christians. The authority the elders possess is from God. They must be guided by all things by the word of God.[47]

A third divergence is in the *life* of an eldership. The Disciples of Christ follow the custom of electing elders for a term, usually of three years, on a rotating pattern. After serving a term, an elder is not qualified for re-election until a year's absence from the board. The philosophy of the "functional pattern" produces elders who "become an integral part of the church life and not a special group set apart from the congregation."[48] Alexander Campbell was of another opinion. He "never had any faith in annual elders, nor in annual elections."[49] When asked should elders resign, and how long should they serve, Leo Boles stated "no one can resign from any work which he is qualified to do and still be pleasing to the Lord." Therefore an elder should "serve as long as he is qualified to serve."[50] The churches of Christ in Great Britain have the custom of ordaining "lay elders" for life. It is felt this "notably strengthens the congregations that cannot find adequately trained ministers."[51]

Guy P. Leavitt, a spokesman for the Christian churches, in 1961 quoted with approval Harding's, *Handbook for Elders and Deacons,* that "a three-year tenure of office is about right."[52] Congregational size is a factor in the development of the rotating board of elders and deacons. Campbell did not have to work with a congregation of one thousand or two thousand members, containing several hundred capable leaders from which to choose.

Restructured Disciples of Christ

The nineteenth-century eldership in most areas of the brotherhood was a ministry of Word, sacrament (baptism and Communion) and pastoral oversight. This has been largely lost in the restructured Disciples of Christ who tend to see the eldership as only one of many functional lay responsibilities. Ronald Osborn has spoken to this situation. "Disciples cannot in good order continue a concept of the office which simultaneously claims that elders are unordained laymen and assigns to them the duties of public ministers."[53] The "layman only" view has not prevailed in the British Isles. The *Report of the Commission on the Ministry* in 1947 states it was "necessary to maintain that ordained Elders, Deacons and Deaconesses are also ministers."

W. B. Blakemore recognizes that the Disciples of Christ have gradually made the office of elder less relevant, consigning it often to the area of Communion in public worship. He lays the blame at the feet of the eldership. "The 'anti-elder' attitude of the twentieth century has many resemblances to the nineteenth century 'anti-clericalism' which was a reaction against earlier abuses of clerical power."[54] I see a different source. The depreciation of the eldership has been the result of an increase of clericalism, a gathering to the "professional" of the prerogatives of ministry. This depreciation of ministry for the eldership may underlie the recent selection of women elders in a few Disciples of Christ churches. Central Christian Church in Enid, Oklahoma, had two women elders in 1972.[55] Daniel Joyce, dean of the Graduate School, Phillips University, believes elder is "not a term that connotes sex." In our present American society he sees no reason to accept the conclusions of the "male-dominated society in the first century." To refuse to consider women as elders makes them remain "second class citizens."[56]

B. The Evangelist

Campbell declared "call those who proclaim the ancient gospel evangelists."[57] He was not willing, however, to equate the evangelist with the role of Timothy and Titus as "agents of the Apostles," for they had a "general superintendence of the affairs of churches." It was a "question of dubious interpretation" to ask if these New Testament duties "may be safely lodged in t e hands of select Evangelists as respects infant communities."[58] Similarity was expressed by W. R. Walker, a national leader of the Christian churches, in his column in the *Christian Standard.*

> In Ephesians 4:11 ff. evangelists are listed among those upon whom special gifts of the Spirit were conferred—undoubtedly a miraculous enduement. An evangelist is not represented as an administrative official. The claim of some modern evangelists that they are successors to Titus . . . is a gratuitous assumption.[59]

It was generally conceded that evangelists had the authority to supervise their converts until they were mature enough to manage their own affairs. Campbell seemingly distinguished between the *Kerygma* and the *Didache.* He saw a difference between teaching and exhorting *in* the church and preaching *to* the unsaved.

The issue has continued in the churches of Christ as to whether or not one can *preach the gospel* to an organized church. This was the underlying tension in the Colley-Ketcherside debate of 1954. Ketcherside's position is seen in the ironic, "You know, it is a strange thing about evangelists in the New Testament. They were always getting ready to go some place else. In the case of Dallas, they are always getting ready to find some place they can settle down in."[60] However, the great majority of the non-instrumental brethren refer to their minister as "evangelist." This has been their answer to the need of a settled ministry and their continued aversion to introducing any term or position they do not identify in the New Testament.

In his *Restoration Handbook,* F. D. Kershner defined the role of evangelist.

> The New Testament evangelist preached the Word, organized churches, superintended the churches as far as superintendence was needed, baptized converts, and, in short, did everything required to build up and nourish the Christian life of the church.[61]

J. W. McGarvey saw the validity of having a "preaching elder" who would give his "whole time to the work." Departing from Campbell's thesis, McGarvey also believed it Scriptural to have an evangelist serve a local congregation. He is "called to the aid of the Eldership."

> He preaches, and takes the leading part in teaching, while the Elders take the secondary part in teaching and supreme control in ruling, making use, however, of whatever wisdom and experience the evangelist may possess, to aid them . . . for in this capacity Timothy labored among the Elders at Ephesus, and Epaphroditus among those at Philippi.[62]

What McGarvey and others of this interpretation overlooked is that the local elders at Ephesus did not call nor did they later control Timothy. Paul sent Timothy to Ephesus and Titus to Crete; and prepared to send Timothy to Philippi (Philippians 2:19). Epaphroditus, a messenger from Philippi, was to be sent back by Paul as a special "brother and fellow worker." Many an article and sermon were dedicated to the proposition that the primitive church had an immutable threefold ministry of elders, deacons, and evangelists, and all functions of ministry must come under one of these offices.

This position has been abandoned by the present Disciples of Christ, and often ignored in practice by the Christian churches.

Area evangelists were used in the early years of the movement. We have already observed Walter Scott's appointment for the Mahoning Baptist Association. In October, 1835, messengers for churches in four counties of Kentucky met to choose evangelists, at a salary of "not less than $500.00" per year. John Smith, Jacob Creath, Jr., B. F. Hall, and J. P. Lancaster were chosen. "It was agreed that the most successful method of operating was for each Evangelist to take a small district of country for the field of his operation, say one or two counties, and cultivate it well."[63] These evangelists assumed many prerogatives that are customarily associated with the role of such as a Methodist bishop.

Professional Evangelists

As the settled pastorate took hold in the majority of the brotherhood churches, the term evangelist was transferred to the itinerate preachers who traveled under their own commission. In this interpretation of this ministry perhaps the first professional evangelist among the Disciples was "singing" Knowles Shaw, born in 1834 in Ohio, dying at age forty-four as a result of a railroad accident. He published five song books and wrote many hymns, including "Bringing in the Sheaves." The first Disciples evangelistic team, a la Moody and Sankey, was J. V. Updike and Hawes. They toured as a team from 1887 to 1894.[64]

The most famous such evangelist was Charles Reign Scoville. He joined the church of Christ in Angola, Indiana, in 1891, and began to preach almost immediately. Scoville was better educated than most leaders of the "sawdust trail," having received AB and MA degrees from Hiram College. More than any other Disciples preacher of his time he held union meetings with denominations. Many of the fundamentalist brethren criticized this approach, claiming such activity prevented him from preaching the "full gospel." He was persuasive. In Jefferson City, Missouri, then a town of fifteen thousand, he closed a seven week union meeting in which four thousand "hit the glory trail."[65] Scoville developed the team approach, using eleven to twelve assistants. Advance agents preceded him to his revival areas preparing the community. It is reported he would preach for an hour to an hour and a half, then exhort for another thirty minutes if he felt the necessity. He was instrumental in forming the National Evangelistic Association, and led in the efforts to create the "Department of Evangelism" of the United Christian Missionary Society (UCMS).

In the Disciples of Christ the use of the traveling evangelist in the church's program has steadily diminished, as they have gone to a more ordered ministry. W. M. Smith in his Reed Lectures at the Disciples of Christ Historical Society stated:

> From several hundred evangelists in 1920, fewer than thirty-five are listed in the current Disciples Year Book (1967). . . . By 1910, virtually every church of Disciples having regular preaching, had a man on the field and, according to studies made in 1925, eighty-five percent lived in parsonages.[66]

The practice of calling the located preacher an evangelist is much less prominent among the Christian churches than in the churches of Christ. Christian church publications have tended to discourage the practice, as evident in the directory that separates the terms of minister and evangelist. Here the term evangelist designates one who is not the pastor of a church. The 1972 *A Directory of the Ministry* lists 216 ministers in the United States and two in Canada who call themselves evangelists. The 1974 edition of the *Directory* shows an increase, to a total of 240. As to evangelistic associations the 1973 *Directory* states: "In March of 1973 . . . a list of some one hundred such associations and agencies was received from Seth Wilson of Ozark Bible College." This *Directory* then names 128 such associations in the United States and four in Canada.[67] The 1972 *Directory* had designated only sixty evangelistic associations in the United States and none in Canada. The number of professional evangelists increased 10 percent from 1972 to 1974, and the number of evangelistic associations more than doubled during the same period.

The Supervising Evangelist

The preoccupation of the movement in the nineteenth century with the local church, and the intensity of allegiance in the churches of Christ and Christian churches in the twentieth century to local autonomy, resulted in an area of production for the evangelist that has not been explored in depth. Robert Milligan recognized a class of evangelists distinct from the eldership and itinerant preachers, as authorized in Ephesians 4:11 and 2 Timothy 2:2. Milligan included such as Barnabas, Mark, Luke, Silas, Gaius, Clement, Aristarchus, and Demas.[68] He met opposition from those viewing the authority of the eldership as supreme. He countered that the principle of love would restrain an evangelist from "interfering with the regular instruction and discipline of a well-ordered and well-instructed congregation." He summed up the practicality of his position:

> What Elders ever complained of the interference of such Evangelists as Alexander Campbell, John T. Johnson, Jacob Creath, William Morton, John Smith, John Rogers, etc.? And what would now be the condition of many congregations throughout the Mississippi Valley had not these eminent Evangelists exercised a timely and judicious watch-care over them?[69]

Certainly Milligan was more frank about the authority exercised by the founding fathers of the movement than they themselves usually were. These men "interfered" in congregations with elected elders, acting as counselors and judges of factions. They assumed for themselves, often without multi-congregational approval, a position similar to that occupied in the 1940's and 1950's by the State Secretaries of the Disciples of Christ. When a preacher edited a paper or journal he, consciously or unconsciously, assumed the role of an area evangelist. In the September, 1845, *Harbinger* Campbell published a list of seventeen current periodicals; and Claude Spencer, curator emeritus of the Historical Society, estimates thirty-five to forty had been published up to that time. Too many unofficial evangelists can spoil the spiritual broth. The 1970 volume *Thoughts on Unity* lists eighty-four such "Christian Magazines."[70]

Whatever the role of the evangelist, the nineteenth-century leaders saw them as "possessed of proper qualification" (I. Errett) by one or more churches. Those traveling without proper credentials were subject to the wrath of the Sage of Bethany.

Some who call themselves evangelists in this our day more strikingly resemble the ostrich than the first preachers. The ostrich drops its egg in the sand, and leaves it to the sun and the sand—to heaven and earth—to take care of it; and then itinerates the desert.[71]

It is interesting that this practice of multi-congregational control has been condoned on the mission fields by both fundamentalists and conservatives. The American missionary has consistently acted as an area evangelist, setting up congregations, serving as preacher and teacher, and giving advice and direction to congregations in a given territory. The missionary has often assumed duties of a denominational bishop. Why this has remained unchallenged might be found beneath racial and psychological undertones.

The idea of area evangelist was transformed into area control of established churches in the second century. Ronald Osborn in encouraging the COCU (Consultation on Church Union) order of "public ministry" has stressed the role of area bishop.

Bishops represent the unity of the church both geographically and historically. The two basic treatises on church order in the New Testament—Acts and the pastoral epistles—depict a number of ministers who served churches across a region . . . bearing responsibility for the faith and life of the believers and for the ordering of the public ministry. The apostles Peter and John, the apostolic missionaries Paul and Barnabas and Silas, the apostolic colleagues Timothy and Titus exercised such episcopal oversight.[72]

C. Deacons and Deaconesses

It has been universally agreed—almost—that the authority for deacons as the third part of the New Testament ministry comes from Acts 6:1-6. Every discussion in the nineteenth century on this subject included its reference. Again, Philippians 1:1 and 1 Timothy 3:8-11 were said to reveal that the deacons, with the bishops, are "a distinct order of ecclesiastical officers."[73] Robert Milligan believed the deacons, as designated in Acts 6:1-6, had the duty "to attend simply to the secular wants and interests of the congregation." He believed the deaconship "conferred no authority whatever, either to teach or to preach, in either the public or the private assembly."[74] F. D. Kershner, in his 1919 *Restoration Handbook,* Series III, merely said the deacons were "the servants in all practical matters of the congregation."

When pastor of a Detroit church, Isaac Errett issued his "Synopsis." It included: "That every church, when fully organized had . . . Deacons who attended to the wants of the poor, and the temporal interests of the church, and assisted likewise in its spiritual ministrations." This includes a spiritual emphasis lacking in Milligan's view.

In 1878, Thomas Munnell followed the broader concept of Errett when he advised, "A deacon's work need not be limited to the secular in interests of religion; for he has many opportunities of doing good."[75]

The leaders looked upon as spiritual fathers of the churches of Christ were fairly consistent in denying the Scripturalness of the position of deaconess. This view was preserved by Daniel Sommer who stated in the *Apostolic Review* in 1910 concerning the threefold ministry: "As we are *unable* to find the scripture which sets forth the qualifications of a deaconess, we should not appoint any for such office." Willis Allen, a preacher for the churches of Christ some sixty years in the twentieth century, stated to the author that he had never known a non-instrumental congregation to have deaconesses. The churches of Christ depart from Alexander Campbell in this regard.

Campbell understood 1 Timothy 3:11 "The *women* likewise must be serious" as referring to deaconesses.[76] Robert Milligan was more expansive:

> The Diaconate of the primitive Church was not confined to male members. Deaconesses were also appointed to attend to the wants of the sick and the needy, especially of their own sex. This is evident from Romans 16:1 and 1 Timothy 5:9-15. This order was continued, in the Greek Church, till about the beginning of the thirteenth century, and it is to be regretted that it was ever discontinued in any Church.[77]

Because of the male-female counterparts of the diaconate, Milligan was sure the office carried certain restrictions. "There is not a single intimation that preaching or teaching is any part of his office." Were it so, "women would never have been made deaconesses."[78] He understood 1 Timothy 2:12 as a divine command from the apostle.

Campbell believed that deacons had a wider ministry than deaconesses. In the *Christian Baptist* he explained that deacons were "public servants of the whole congregation." Deaconesses were "female public servants who officiate amongst the females."[79] The extent of services is not fully known, but when the Poca Street Church of Baltimore was organized in 1833 it included deaconesses. Campbell in 1850 had dedicated the new facility, and D. S. Burnet became pastor there in 1864.

The deaconesses have come into their own sphere in the Disciples of Christ only in the last quarter century. Even among the more liberal elements of the Disciples of Christ the deaconesses are used primarily "to prepare the elements of Communion, call on shut-ins and do a few other chores around the church. Very rarely have they ever served in the regular Communion service on Sunday morning."[80]

The role of the deacon developed differently among the non-instrumental brethren than that of the Christian churches and Disciples of Christ. It became customary in the latter two groups for deacons to be in charge of certain "secular" matters about the church, as finances, housekeeping and repair. Not so among the churches of Christ. Here the deacons work under the eldership in all matters. As late as 1967 the editor of the *Gospel Advocate* reminded the churches, "It is the deacon's work to serve, not to exercise the oversight."[81] A newer, and seemingly minority view, is expressed by Robert Barrett in *Mission* in 1972. "We must realize that the diaconate and the eldership are different areas on the same plane rather than one's being a step upwards from the other."[82] J. D. Murch quotes an interesting interpretation in a proposed ordination service for deacons.

> The deacons have been described as "the living bond of union between the congregation and its elders; taken from the bosom of the community; chosen entirely by the people themselves; intimately acquainted with their wants; and thus admirably qualified to assist the elders with counsel and action in all their official duties.[83]

In this century several scholars, including Stephen England

and William Robinson, have understood Acts 6:1-6 in a wider field. They reason that if the officers selected in this section had a title at all, it was probably *elder*. Acts 11:30 refers to the elders of the Jerusalem church, and there is no other prior election or selection stated (See Acts 15:4). William J. Moore observes:

> The term *Diakonas* is not applied to the seven and while the infinitive *diakonein* (Acts 6:2) is used with reference to their work of "serving" tables, the noun *diakonia* is employed in Acts 6:4 to refer not to their labors but to those of the apostles.[84]

If this approach is correct, then Acts 6 becomes a key to ministry more than a proof text for the diaconate. This point being that the work of the apostle was a specific ministry and not a general serve-all administration. The setting is Acts 5:42; "And every day in the temple and at home they did not cease teaching and preaching Jesus as the Christ." Social concern is integral for the church, but it is not equal to "ministry of the word." The movement perhaps should evaluate this distinction—if one there be—between ministry and administration.

A group of scholars largely identified with the Disciples of Christ have suggested that the nineteenth-century leadership was guilty of formulating universal applications from particular incidents. Such is seen in absolutizing the polity situation in the pastoral epistles and Acts 14:23, to the exclusion of organizational conformation in other epistles. This approach stresses the folly of trying to "blueprint" the spontaneity and variability of the New Testament.

Notes to Chapter 3

1. James E. Craig, "Who Are the Disciples of Christ," *Look* (November 30, 1954), p. 104.

2. W. E. Garrison, *Heritage and Destiny* (St. Louis: Bethany Press, 1961), p. 73.

3. *Report of the Commission on the Ministry,* p. 5.

4. W. B. Blakemore, *The Scroll* (Autumn, 1953), p. 32.

5. W. B. Blakemore, "The Eldership," *The Christian* (April 25, 1965), p. 30.

6. *Millennial Harbinger* (December, 1839), p. 573.

7. A. Campbell, "Epaphras—No. III," *Millennial Harbinger* (October, 1832), p. 501.

8. A. Campbell, *The Christian System,* 1835 (Standard Publishing, reprint), p. 60.

9. *Millennial Harbinger* (April, 1840), p. 182.

10. *Millennial Harbinger* (November, 1856), p. 618.

11. A. Campbell, *The Christian System* (reprint), p. 61.

12. Henry Bettenson, ed., *Documents of the Christian Church,* 2nd ed. (London: Oxford University Press, 1967), p. 66.

13. A. Campbell, *The Christian System* (reprint) cf. pp. 80-82, also Winebrenner (ed.), *History of all the Religious Denominations in the United States* (second, improved and portrait edition) (Harrisburg, Pa.: published by editor, 1849), p. 229.

Millennial Harbinger (November, 1851), p. 638.

Christian Messenger (July, 1843), p. 67.

New Christian Quarterly (October, 1893), p. 435.

14. F. M. Green, *The Christian Minister's Manual* (St. Louis: John Burns Publisher, 1883), p. 19.

15. *The Christian Quarterly* (January, 1872), p. 83.

16. *Ibid.,* pp. 78-81.

17. W. E. Garrison, *Heritage and Destiny,* p. 73.

18. A. Campbell, *Christian Baptist,* Vol. II (September 6, 1824) reprint, p. 37.

19. Madison Evans, *Biographical Sketches of the Pioneer Preachers of Indiana* (Philadelphia: J. Challen and Sons, 1862), p. 5.

20. James D. Murch, *The Free Church* (Restoration Press, 1966), p. 79.

21. D. Ray Lindley, *Apostle of Freedom* (St. Louis: Bethany Press, 1957), cf. p. 131.

22. R. Richardson, *Memoirs of Alexander Campbell,* Vol. II (reprint), p. 603.

23. A. Campbell, *Christian Baptist* (June, 1826), Vol. III (reprint), p. 216.

24. *Ibid.,* (October, 1824), Vol. II (reprint), p. 54.

25. *Ibid.,* p. 53.

26. Ronald E. Osborn, *In Christ's Place: Christian Ministry in Today's World* (St. Louis: Bethany Press, 1967), p. 257.

27. A. Campbell, *Christian Baptist* (September, 1829), Vol. VII (reprint), p. 37.

28. J. W. McGarvey, *A Treatise on the Eldership* (1870) (Murfreesboro, Tenn.: T. DeHoff Publications, 1962 reprint ed.), p. 56.

29. *Ibid.,* cf. p. 87.

30. Robert Milligan, *Scheme of Redemption,* pp. 328, 329.

31. W. R. Walker, "The Counselor's Question Box," *Christian Standard* (July 5, 1958), p. 384.

32. "Noble Answers," *The Lookout* (January 7, 1973), p. 6.

33. "Concerning Church Government," *Apostolic Review* (1910), p. 1.

34. H. Leo Boles, *The Eldership of the Churches of Christ* (Nashville: Gospel Advocate Co., n.d.), p. 27.

35. *Ibid.,* pp. 30-32.

36. Flavel L. Colley, ed., *Colley-Ketcherside Debate* (Dallas: Flavel L. Colley, 1954), p. 23.

37. R. Richardson, *Memoirs of Alexander Campbell,* Vol. II (1868; reprint, Cincinnati: Standard Publishing), p. 599.

38. "Discipline of the Church," *Abilene Christian Church Bible Lectures,* 1921-1922, p. 102.

39. *Ibid.,* "Mutual Edification in the Church of Christ," p. 85.

40. "Work of Elders," *Abilene Christian College Lectures,* 1946 (Old Paths Book Club, 1946), p. 164.

41. Louise King, *Memoirs of David King,* 1895? (College Press: Restoration Reprint Library, reprint), p. 290.

42. *Ibid.,* p. 275.

43. J. W. McGarvey, *A Treatise on the Eldership,* p. 89.

44. *The Eldership of the Churches of Christ* (Nashville: Gospel Advocate Co., n. d.), p. 37. See H. E. Winkler, *The Eldership* (Nashville: Williams Printing Co., 1950), pp. 38, 39.

45. "Shepherd the Church," *Gospel Advocate* (September 28, 1967), p. 610.

46. "A Chat With Chet," *The Christian* (June 4, 1972), p. 32.

47. David Lipscomb, *Queries and Answers* (Nashville: Gospel Advocate Co., reprint 1963), p. 152.

48. *You Are an Elder* (Home and State Missions Planning Council of the Disciples of Christ).

49. *Millennial Harbinger,* (July, 1844), p. 322.

50. *The Eldership of the Church of Christ,* p. 38.

51. "The Christian Ministry," *Doctrines of the Christian Faith* (Study Committee of the World Convention of Churches of Christ (Disciples) 1956), p. 9.

52. "How to Be a Better Church Officer," *Christian Standard* (October 21, 1961), p. 668.

53. Ronald E. Osborn, *In Christ's Place,* p. 258.

54. "The Christian Task and the Church's Ministry," *The Revival of the Churches,* Vol. III (St. Louis: Bethany Press, 1963), p. 155.

55. *The Christian* (September 17, 1972), p. 8.

56. *Ibid.,* (June 4, 1972), pp. 4, 5.

57. A. Campbell, "Official Names and Titles," *Christian Baptist* Vol. VII (1829), p. 48.

58. A. Campbell, *The Christian System* (reprint), p. 63.

59. W. R. Walker, "The Counselor's Question Box," *Christian Standard* (September 27, 1958), p. 554.

60. Flavel L. Colley, ed., *Colley-Ketcherside Debate,* p. 21.

61. *The Restoration Handbook,* Series III (Cincinnati: Standard Publishing, 1919), p. 24.

62. J. W. McGarvey, *A Treatise on the Eldership,* p. 66.

63. *Life of Elder John Smith* (reprint), p. 439.

64. *Christian Standard* (March 11, 1905), cf. pp. 395, 396.

65. *The Christian-Evangelist* (December 15, 1915).

66. William Martin Smith, *Servants Without Hire* (Nashville: The Disciples of Christ Historical Society, 1968), p. 70.

67. *A Directory of the Ministry of the Undenominational Fellowship of Christian Churches and Churches of Christ; 1974,* (Springfield, Illinois: Specialized Christian Services), p. F-37.

68. R. Milligan, *Scheme of Redemption* (reprint), p. 310.

69. *Ibid.,* p. 311.

70. Stanley Paregien, ed., *Thoughts on Unity* (St. Louis: Mission Messenger, n.d.), pp. 317-319.

71. *Millennial Harbinger* (1835), p. 527.

72. Ronald E. Osborn, *In Christ's Place,* p. 243.

73. R. Milligan, *Scheme of Redemption* (reprint), p. 339.

74. *Ibid.,* p. 341.

75. Thomas Munnell, *The Care of All the Churches* (St. Louis: Christian Publishing Co., 1878), p. 114.

76. *Millenniel Harbinger,* Vol. II (1845), p. 15.

77. R. Milligan, *The Scheme of Redemption,* p. 343.

78. *Millennial Harbinger,* (November, 1855), p. 626.

79. A. Campbell, *Christian Baptist,* Vol. VII (1829), pp. 47, 48.

80. J. Daniel Joyce, "The Mutual Ministry of Men and Women," *The Christian* (June 4, 1972), p. 4.

81. *Gospel Advocate* (September 28, 1967), p. 610.

82. *Mission* (July, 1972), p. 9.

83. James DeForest Murch, *Christian Minister's Manual* (Cincinnati: Standard Publishing, 1937), p. 168.

84. William J. Moore, *The New Testament Concept of the Ministry* (St. Louis: Bethany Press, 1956), p. 41.

4

the development of an ordered ministry

The Settled Pastor Controversy

The early reformers were wary of a settled pastorate, which symbolized the professional clergyman and his "kingdom." "They were determined that preachers would travel from place to place, doing the work of an evangelist, and that the local 'bishop' should be the head of the churches."[1] Campbell described the kind of minister the movement must avoid:

> A hireling is one who prepares himself for the office of a "preacher" or "minister," as a mechanic learns a trade, and who obtains a license from a congregation, convention, presbytery, pope, or diocesan bishop, as a preacher or minister, and agrees by the day or sermon, month or year, for stipulated reward. . . . He learns the art and mystery of making a sermon, or a prayer, as a man learns the art of making a boot or a shoe.[2]

The reformers considered the "one man system" unscriptural. There was godly resentment against any system that implied authority over the local elders. Widespread argument of "one man power" came to the front around 1850, and has remained with the churches of Christ to this day. Before 1850 the great majority of preachers traveled a circuit and held "protracted meetings." David Lipscomb wrote in the *Gospel Advocate* in 1873, "After a church is planted the idea of retaining a man to preach constantly for that congregation is foreign to the whole scope of Biblical teaching."[3]

Moses E. Lard had a sermon entitled "My Church." It began, "I own no church, and in this am most unpardonably unlike the *city pastors.*"[4] In 1954 Carl Ketcherside was mirroring the attitude of Lipscomb when he affirmed that one cannot "locate the scripture authorizing a congregation with elders hiring a preacher to preach to the church."[5]

J. W. McGarvey in his 1870 *Treatise on the Eldership* expressed a similar view, as he discussed the meaning of "pastor" in Ephesians 4:11. "The evidence that this term designated the *overseers* or *elders* is conclusive." *Poimaino,* to McGarvey, meant, *"to do the work* of a shepherd."[6] He declared that for the King James version to translate the word seven times as *feed* was "a very inadequate translation."[7] It gave evangelists the wrong impression of public teaching and led to the mistake of their considering themselves *pastors* of churches. Yet, in his *Autobiography* McGarvey claimed receiving a "call" to the Lexington, Kentucky, church in 1861, and added: "This was the beginning of a ministry of five years during which the church grew from being the fourth in size to be the largest in the city."[8] Again, it would seem that the theological position of a subservient "preacher" was supplanted by a pastor-in-fact ministry.

Ben Franklin feared the germ of clericalism as it "must" be hidden in the settled pastorate. This determination to destroy the "evil of the one man system" was continued by Tolbert Fanning and David Lipscomb. At this same time the *Evangelist,* under J. H. Garrison, and the *Standard,* under Isaac Errett, were siding with the planted pastorate. In *Lard's Quarterly,* Errett placed an announcement concerning the Detroit congregation and identified himself "Isaac Errett, Pastor."[9]

The small country churches did not have a pressing need for a settled pastor. As the frontier grew up and the cities developed, a corresponding need for a professional minister developed. There was a considerable period of adjustment in lines of authority and personality conflicts. Thus the "located preachers" in the 1850-1880 period were hardly located at all. Isaac Errett called attention to this problem:

> It strikes me that our people are exceedingly *fickle* about their pastors, if it can be said they have any fixed ideas of a pastorate. Scarcely do they call one, and he has hardly time to reconnoiter the field, when they desire a change. A year is the general rule, and many, when they begin a year are uncertain they will be satisfied enough to justify a continuance through it.[10]

During the 1858 Cincinnati meeting of the American Christian Missionary Society (ACMS), Errett bemoaned there were "no pastors in cities such as Washington, New York, Baltimore, Lexington, Peoria; and that Philadelphia, Cincinnati, St. Louis, Richmond, Nashville, and Springfield, Illinois, "have each but one pastor." A current church of Christ scholar has taken issue with Errett's evaluation of Disciples strength in these areas. Harrell states:

> The lack of pastors was more the result of deep-seated prejudices against the "pastor system" than an overwhelming absence of churches in these Western cities.[11]

The man who most clearly saw the need for a professional ministry in the second half of the nineteenth century was Thomas Munnell. His *The Care of All The Churches* in 1878 was to that date the best expression published in this field. Munnell was sure the Scriptures taught that the ministry in the "care of all the churches" has the work of "the establishing, the feeding and the protection of the church of God, including a wholesome and scriptural discipline and culture."[12] Alexander Campbell was not without witness to a teaching elder or preaching elder. He could say in 1850: "To teach Christ is primarily the work of a pastor, or feeder of the flock: therefore he is called teacher as well as pastor."[13] Again, Campbell is observed in his later writings changing the meanings he gave to such terms as "evangelist" and "pastor." In his earlier *Christian Baptist* days he identified the "pastor" with an abolished supernatural ministry (see *Christian Baptist,* Vol. II, October 4, 1824). As noted above, he came to recognize the need of a pastoral ministry and considered such a specializing elder or bishop. This bishop, giving much of his time and effort to the congregation, is worthy of financial remuneration.

Today the churches of Christ still guard against any concept of pyramid control from the preacher, as is practiced uniformly in the Disciples of Christ. J. D. Thomas describes the almost universal situation:

> When elders employ a preacher, they "control" his actions and maintain full responsibility, yet they delegate to him a wide range of authority in making decisions relative to his work. But here nobody feels they have surrendered control.[14]

Leo Boles had stated the proposition a few decades earlier. "It is a perversion of God's order to speak of the preacher as 'the pastor.' He may not even be *a* pastor, and surely he cannot be *the* pastor."[15] In 1913 W. E. Ramsey, writing in the

Apostolic Review, attacked the pastor system with more than customary vigor. He cried:

> I believe that all the "humanisms," divisions, strifes, jealousies, disappointments, hurts, heartaches and downright spiritual murder can be laid at the door of this one man in the church—if indeed he be in it. Of all the chicanery and politics in religion, I found it there.[16]

Whatever development of a systematic professional ministry has been made in the past fifty years in the churches of Christ has been done on a practical basis, without any expressed theological foundation. By theological evaluation the pastor of a church is officially an elder or an evangelist and is a servant of the eldership of a local congregation.

The Emerging Pastor System

Thomas Munnell saw the limitations of the polity and system elucidated by Campbell in the writing of the *Christian Baptist.* He saw the brotherhood as failing to restore primitive Christianity in the Pauline area of "teaching from house to house." He complained: "We call a brother to preach for us on Sunday and go home. The members are not visited. The pulpit is everything with us, while the 'going about doing good,' as Jesus did, is not in our practice at all, except in our city churches."[17] More time was required than a traveling evangelist could give "for setting disabled congregations in good order." Without depreciating the eldership, Munnell could point out: "How unreasonable to expect brethren who have been elected to office in the church without any experience in such matters, to conduct them aright simply because they are men of character and piety."[18] Others did not share this view, as evidenced by the complaint of Robert Graham, later president of the College of the Bible, deploring "the growing disposition to recognize the distinction of clergy and laity in our churches."[19]

Historically, the first church leader to speak of a single bishop over the presbyters and deacons of a congregation was Ignatius of Antioch, who died about A.D. 115. He seemed to compare the role of bishop to that of the elders with Christ's leadership over the apostles. He makes the analogy of Christ, apostles, and universal church to that of Bishop, Elders, and congregation. From the "Letters to the Ephesians" comes:

> For Jesus Christ, our inseparable life is the mind of the Father, just as the bishops who are appointed all over the world are in the mind of Jesus Christ.[20]

Ignatius sought through the bishops some sure, fixed authority to combat the growing Gnosticism in Asia Minor. He wrote to the Smyrnaeans: "You must all follow the bishop, as Jesus Christ followed the Father, and you must follow the board of elders as you would the apostles."[21] T. M. Lindsay says church history bears out the growth of a "president elder" or "pastor elder" in the early church. "The president, sometimes called the pastor, but usually the bishop, became gradually the centre of all the ecclesiastical life of the local Christian church and the one potent office-bearer."[22]

The point of this excursion into the apostolic age is that in approximately the same span of time the Disciples in America went from the pristine elder, deacon, evangelist concept to the "pastor elder" polity in the local church. The customary services and procedures of the public minister are largely the same among the three segments of the historic movement. Theologically, among the churches of Christ he is the agent of the eldership; for the Christian churches he is a co-laborer with the elders and the pastor-administrator for the congregation; for the Disciples of Christ he is a professional clergyman distinct from the "lay ministry of the eldership."

The British churches of Christ in the nineteenth century were influenced largely by the thinking of Alexander Campbell and David King. King was committed to following the "pattern" of the New Testament, and pushed his ideas vigorously. A broader insight came with the establishment of Overdale College in 1920, and the British expanded their concept of ministry beyond that of the local officials of elder and deacon.

There was a continuing dialogue concerning the scope and activity of the ministry in the annual conferences which resulted in a study Commission being formed in 1947. The Commission produced the Report on the Ministry which was published in the 1954 *Conference Year Book*. William Mander says the effect was: "the long cherished conviction that Churches of Christ possess the only form of Ministry consistent with New Testament practice was abandoned."[23] The report stressed the New Testament emphasis upon *episcope,* pastoral oversight, and *diakonia,* service. This was an admission that the New Testament was not so detailed, so patterned as to "give a complete answer to every question which may arise." Recognizing the work of the Holy Spirit in the church, the report could not declare that any one form of ministry was of the *esse* of the church. Today, as one result of this evolvement, the British churches have deleted largely the word "evangelist," because of the popular concept of an itinerant revival preacher. "Minister" has become the accepted term.

New Directions

A decisive volume released in 1973, *The Imperative Is Leadership,* gives a report on ministerial development among the Disciples of Christ. It recognizes the "corporate ministry" of the membership. It emphasizes also the "ministry of the laity" having reference to the "elders, deacons, and deaconesses in the total life of the congregation."[24] Carroll Cotten adds a sentence that certainly would cause Campbell gyrations in the grave:

> From Alexander Campbell to the present, the Disciples have always sought a well-educated leadership, both lay and *clergy"* (emphasis mine).[25]

Cotten acknowledges a present serious problem among the Disciples of Christ: "There are significant differences in expectation regarding a wide spectrum of church life and style of ministerial leadership between laity and pastoral ministers."[26] He sees one major schism of thought in the role of the ministry.

> Ministers tend to view their role as leading and equipping the laity for their ministry to the world. Laity tend to view the minister as *their chaplain* employed to preach, teach, and comfort them.[27]

Here is tacit recognition that the present professional ministry of the Disciples of Christ has embarked upon a role, rightly or wrongly, that is misunderstood by the fellowship. This misunderstanding has led to frustration and reduced corporate ministry. The recent organization of the Academy of Parish Clergy will continue present trends and profoundly affect the theology of the pastoral ministry in the coming years.

Several charts and tables in *The Imperative Is Leadership* give comparatives that may reflect the changed concept of the professional ministry. Between 1961 and 1971 the participating membership of the Disciples of Christ decreased 35.6 percent. At the same time pastors of congregations went from 6,144 to 5,328, a 13.3 percent decrease. Again this period saw a decrease of seminarians from 734 to 584, a drop of 20.4 percent. Baptisms for the Disciples of Christ in 1961 numbered 46,479, but declined 50 percent to 23,120 in 1972. Cotten makes this evaluation: "The basic trend remains the same: decline in virtually every category of the dimensions of the church."[28] Many Disciples of Christ ministers who attended seminary with me over twenty years ago have left the pastorate for regional and administrative positions. The frank reply to questions has usually been that the action and power of the Disciples is not in the pastorate. This is a malaise that must be resolved if the congregational level of the church is to become strong enough to support the regional and national manifestations.

Increasingly the term "priest" has entered the vocabulary of the professional ministry of the Disciples of Christ. It is usually associated with direction of public worship and "administering the sacraments." This appears to be an evolvement of Stone's position among the nineteenth-century Christians. Ronald Osborn has suggested that the denomination think through the nature of the eldership, whether it will be a "purely policy-making office" or be ministerial. "Where the office is not understood as ministerial, elders should refrain from the ministerial responsibility of presiding over holy communion."[29] W. B. Blakemore appears to be an isolated voice among the Disciples of Christ leadership in ruing the decline of the ministerial duties of the eldership. He considers it a "tragedy" that "with the emergence of the professional ministry, we have fallen into a 'one-man' concept of the ministry." The result is that the eldership has "lost their understanding of themselves as overseers of the general ministerial functions."[30]

Considerable evolution has taken place in the Disciples of Christ theology of the ministry in the past twenty years. The result has been a restructured, tiered ministry to correspond to a restructured, tiered church. There emerges the parish clergyman, the regional minister, and the general ministry. The church and its ministry have been arranged in a connectional system to correspond to the ecclesiastical and political (in its generic sense) structures of American life. William Howland, Jr., articulated this concept in 1965 by asserting, "The image of the minister, associated with the words 'priest,' 'preacher' and 'pastor' as they were used from the time of the Reformation to the early decades of this century, is no longer existent or valid."[31] The prior image of "preacher" and "pastor" must give way to the more inclusive field of the "pastoral director" and "enabler." This field is too broad for the traditional role, and "his energies are no longer simply directed to the 'saving of souls.' "[32]

This concept seeks a "maturity" for the corporate ministry of the fellowship to "enable" them to extend their ministry throughout the community and attend to its social diseases. The practical result often has been social activism, participation in labor disputes, involvement in welfare and racial conflicts. Through wisdom or lack of it, the great majority of the "pew" has not comprehended this new "parson" and his mission. The next decade will judge whether a sufficiently positive contribution has been made by this ministry which seeks, in the words of W. E. Garrison, to be "intelligently devoted to the whole task of the whole church."[33]

Among the Conservatives

In a sermon "The Fellowship," Isaac Errett talked of "our *ministers* and *elders* and leading men" (emphasis mine),[34] practical admission of the ordered ministry. The question among the Christian churches has been how to Scripturally classify this creature. W. R. Walker saw an analogy with the Jewish synagogue. "Every synagogue had one or more rulers, probably chosen from the 'elders.' The ruler presided at the public services, selected the reader of the Scriptures for the day, and named the 'preacher.' He was the moderator of the assembly."[35] From this position, there is a logical transfer to the Christian "synagogue" and its "located minister." By arrangement with the congregation the minister "becomes an administrative member of the 'pastors' or 'elders' of a congregation, exercising the functions or performing the duties they may delegate to him. He acts in their behalf, and under their direction."[36] The minister has his "commission . . . from Jesus Christ" but the local congregation has "contracted for his time" as a servant, a *diakonas*.[37]

D. S. Burnet was an early advocate of the pastor system. His first pastorate was at age twenty in 1828 in Dayton, Ohio. His association with the Disciples began that year when he and James Challen organized the Christian church at Eighth and Walnut in Cincinnati. The Campbell-Owen debate was held in Cincinnati in 1829, and Judge Jacob Burnet, D. S.'s uncle, was moderator. W. T. Moore said of Burnet's work:

> Brother Burnet saw that pastoral labor must be done in the churches, and especially the city churches, before they could ever reach that spiritual growth which would enable them to exert a proper influence on the world. . . . He did not argue that the pastoral office is a distinct office from the eldership, but that it is a part of the work of the eldership.[38]

J. W. McGarvey also approved of a "preaching elder" in the board of elders. The preaching elder "proclaims the gospel to the world in the public assembly, and takes the leading part in the instruction of the congregation. He gives his whole time to the work, and lives of the gospel which he preaches."[39]

Not all the conservative leadership was sure the professional minister fit easily into the office of elder. The British Disciple David King, a leading evangelist by 1848, was quite frank about the problem. "The popular pastor, or minister, is a creature of whom no trace can be found in the apostolic writings. . . . His office, so far as the New Testament enables us to trace its origin, arises from limiting the evangelist to, and it perpetuating him in one church."[40] Concerning the nineteenth-century attitude toward the ministry, W. R. Warren gave this evaluation: from indifference (1809-1823), to hostility (1823-1830), to neglect (1830-1840), to kindly interest (1840-1870), to increasing concern (1870-1895).

In the first decade of the twentieth century, W. E. Moore expressed on many occasions that the New Testament ministry was more functional than formalized. He was not troubled by a "blueprint" obligation. F. D. Kershner admitted also: "It is further conceded by most authorities that there is no form of church government laid down in the New Testament as absolutely mandatory upon Christians."[41] The first half of the twentieth century had an "increasing concern" for educational and financial elevation of the ordered ministry. Accent was more on function than on form, and service rather than structure.

An article in the 1971 *Christian Standard* argues that "the minister" of a church is without Scriptural basis, and that it is "neither wholesome nor refreshing" to try to twist a few Bible phrases to find support for our professional position. The argument is that since we have imperfect Christians and inadequate elders, "why not admit that our modern concept of 'the ministry' is not to be found in the Bible?" Boyce Mouton's thesis is that "the minister" should consider himself the "key man" in developing the corporate ministry of the membership.[42] This view is a minority expression among the Christian churches who believe that their ministry needs to have Scriptural precedence, for the satisfaction of the plea and the "restoration of the primitive Church." Donald Nash expressed the need for the churches to find a common name for the professional minister. "Minister" was too general. He concluded: "the position of the located preacher is in the New Testament, and that the New Testament term for it is *pastor,* and that *pastor* is not just a synonym for *elder.* The pastor is listed in Ephesians 4:11 as one of the officers in the New Testament church, along with apostles, evangelists, and teachers."[43]

The conservative wing of the movement has not grappled with the totality of ministry as have the Disciples of Christ in the last quarter century. Expressions have been isolated and fractional, rarely laying a broad theological foundation. The lack of attention to this field is noticeable in the *Report of the Commission on Restudy.* The Commission was created by the 1934 International Convention. For fifteen years of activity it used the "thoughtful services of thirty-nine leaders of our brotherhood life." Sixty-three papers were presented for discussion through the years, three being on the ministry. However, in the thirty-eight-page report authorized by the 1948 International Convention, *there is not one single sentence referring to the ministry.*

The Disciples of Christ

In a 1961 address before the Kansas City International Convention of Christian Churches, Hollis Lee Turley, president of the Pension Fund, saw that the successful mission of the church "rests very largely with the ministry." He cautioned that since the "ministry reflects the strength and the weakness of the church" the "cause of the ministry . . . becomes one of the major concerns of the decade."[44]

For the past twenty-five years the Disciples of Christ have directed their "establishment" writings and productions into areas of form and structure. The ministry has been structured in terminology (clergymen), direction (churchmanship), and relationship (parish, regional, general). Charles R. Gresham, then professor at Emmanuel School of Religion, Milligan College, Tennessee, described this result to the approach of the type of modern minister: "The secular minister of a secular gospel to the secular city preaches with no sense of authority—if he preaches at all."[45] One fact is evident: the "saving of souls" has been numerically reduced in half in the last decade in the congregations of the Disciples of Christ. But then the "saving of souls" is a vocal concern of congregations with a theological outlook of fundamentalism or conservatism.

The Disciples of Christ trend is to seek increasing "professionalization of the ministry." The purpose is to counteract the isolation of the pastor "operating independently from other clergy." The designation for this new mutual accountability is "collegiality." The hope is to provide the Disciples clergy an alternative to the "authoritarian" psychosis and give the ordered ministry "psychological and social roots amid a changing society."[46] Perhaps Kenneth Johnson was prophetic when he stated, during the St. Louis International Convention in 1967, that approval by the Disciples of Christ of the *Provisional Design for the Restructure of the Brotherhood* would "set up a new order of ministry."

Apostolic Succession

The doctrine of Holy Orders with continuity back to the apostles has found no advocates among the churches of Christ and Christian churches, and few among the Disciples of Christ. All the nineteenth-century brotherhood "knew from the Scriptures that the Apostles were of a divine order with a special mission and that they could not and did not perpetuate their kind."[47] Campbell was quite vocal on this. He described apostolic succession as "essentially papistical," in that it advocated "authority in the church from an order distinct from the church."[48] To him, such a system carried the seeds of abuse and deterioration and could be traced through history by the trail of blood of Christian saints. Beginning with the first volume of the *Christian Baptist* he used such expressions as "the haughty pontiff that sits upon the throne of an imaginary St. Peter." He wrote that for two centuries "there is not one word intimating that Peter was ever Bishop of Rome." He saw in the Bible rather "clear and explicit proof that Peter lived and died an *Apostle,* and was never bishop of any particular see."[49] Campbell could not tolerate a theory that stated or implied exclusive channels of grace, which is the foundation of sacramentalism, and thus sacerdotalism.

Isaac Errett took substantially the same position. Peter himself set qualifications for the office of apostle (Acts 1) which men of later generations could not fulfill. Apostolic writings give no indication that the apostles were the first of an order of succession.[50] Peter's "keys" of Matthew 16:16 were to be compared to Matthew 18:18, said Ashley S. Johnson. He admitted that the keys were "preeminently given to Peter," but saw also that "in an exalted sense the other apostles had the same power."[51] Many writers explained that Peter's keys turned the doors to the kingdom on Pentecost, and at the house of Cornelius (Acts 10:34-48). Thereafter these doors have remained open to all who would enter by commitment to the crucified Lord. The British *Report of the Commission on the Ministry* continued the traditional approach. Viewing the history of the ministry in the early centuries, it concluded, "we find that no attempt was made to perpetuate an order called 'apostles.' Further, the order of prophets appears to have died out in the second century."[52]

T. Munnell believed, as did many others, in Biblical apostolic succession: "A restoration of primitive Christianity, and hold that this constitutes the true succession to the apostles."[53] All Christian preachers are in this line of succession, if they work for the "conversion of the world and the edification of the church."[54] Every major voice in the nineteenth century, and most of all the leaders in the first half of the twentieth century, of all segments of the movement, repudiated the idea of official grace being handed down by superior to inferior, with its resulting inherent powers. J. D. Murch expresses a similar idea in pointing out, "True ministers of the gospel are successors of the apostles—not in the sense that they are clothed with apostolic authority, but in the sense that they succeed to the apostolic work of preaching 'the unsearchable riches of Christ.' "[55]

When the Kentucky Synod tried to enforce its decrees upon Barton Stone and his associates in 1803, they responded with an *Apology for Renouncing the Jurisdiction of the Synod of Kentucky.* From where did the synod's authority come? Was it from the See of Rome and its line of succession?—yet Luther denounced it as a corrupt system. From Calvin and Luther?—how could their ordination then carry sacramental grace? To the synod went the challenge: "We would be glad to see authentic testimonials of the spiritual genealogy proving their orderly descent from the Apostles of Christ."[56] The denominational appeals to continuity were a "thorn in the flesh" to the rise of the movement.

Brotherhood literature of the middle nineteenth century shows recurring attacks on the Roman Catholic theory of ministerial authority. All over Protestant America in this period there was great agitation over the dangers of "Popery" and "Romanism." Campbell pointed up the "lies of Romanism" that had held much of the Christian world in spiritual slavery. It was not surprising when Walter Scott penned: "Popery is the perfect Pandora's box from which have issued all the evils that have afflicted Christendom for the last 1,000 years."[57] The churches of Christ and the Christian churches carried traces of this absolutism into the twentieth century. For example, advertisements for the Christian churches would occasionally publicize the evangelistic efforts of reformed Roman Catholic priests. Again, the bookshelves of a church of Christ center will reveal presentations of "turn-coat" tales of former clergymen.

Up to the 1950's there was general agreement in the movement that episcopal succession threatened the New Testament position. Continuity with the first century was expressed as a pursuit of truth. Power was present in the Lord and His Book. An 1845 article in the *Harbinger* expressed this idea. "Both Christ and the Apostles are now *in the church*–the first by his spirit, the last by their writings—as they were in the apostolic days."[58] Second Timothy 2:2 was used as a key to the issue, demonstrating a succession of "consecrated personality" and not "official order." Continuity was in the reproduction of the spirit and devotion to Christ that was the leaven of the primitive church. Continuity was in the teachings of the Master. This was part of the plea for a restoration of the New Testament church.

Hans Kung, the Roman Catholic scholar, has expressed a view not unsimilar to this of the Disciples:

> The fundamental "apostolic succession" is therefore that of the Church itself and of each individual Christian. It must consist of an objective keeping of faith with the apostles, which must be concretely realized anew over and over again.[59]

This is accomplished by "apostolic testimony" in the New Testament and "apostolic ministry," the evangelizing of the world.

Campbell, in his theory of succession, distinguished between the ministerial office and the officer himself.

> There is no succession in the office—that the office and the officer must be regarded as two distinct things—that the office is one and indivisible—and that the succession is in the officers and not in the office.[60]

This emphasis was recognized by Charles Clayton Morrison as he made this observation more than one hundred years later: "Virtually all our ministers are ordained in the succession of ministers, that is, they are ordained by other ministers who were themselves ordained by other ministers." This succession of ministers has deep significance to the candidate, and "few ministers would feel that they had been properly set apart to the ministry unless some other minister or ministers participated in their ordination."[61]

A noticeable change has taken place in the last quarter century among the Disciples of Christ. Restructure and participation of the Disciples of Christ in COCU have brought these new concepts to a focus. At Los Angeles in 1962 the International Convention passed Resolution #50, authorizing the Council on Christian Unity to participate in COCU. George G. Beazley, the guiding force of the council, stated a few months later that he believed the "Disciples should not have too much difficulty accepting the 1888 Lambeth Quadrilateral" of the Episcopal church. One of the four points deemed essential for unity in this document is acceptance of the historic episcopate.

The "Preamble" to the *Provisional Design for the Christian Church* (Disciples of Christ) contains a sentence that is subject to episcopal interpretation. "Within the universal church we receive the gift of ministry and the light of scripture." The first drafts carried the phrase "Within the Church," capitalizing *church,* but not Scripture. The Disciples' historic position is the contrary: within the New Testament Scriptures we find the principles of the church. The acceptance of authoritative tradition would include the second- and third-century concepts of the bishopric, being separated from the laity, and in fact the essence of the church. The brotherhood stance of the ministry as being part of the church and representative of the congregation is bypassed in the restructured Disciples of Christ. Restructure recognizes "ordained ministers who have ministerial standing . . . in accordance with the policies established by the General Assembly."

Elements in the Disciples of Christ have come to a doctrine of the ministry based upon orders, grades, and authority, with an affinity for the historic episcopate. This position is defended on the ground that "Restoration—whether of the last century, or of eighteen centuries before that—is a delusion."[62] The concept is that the church, as a soaring bird, cannot return to the shell from which it was hatched. The Voice commands as it did to Moses: "Speak to my people that they go forward." No longer for the Disciples of Christ is there any relevancy in the New Testament as a *blueprint* for church order and ministry. Perhaps a majority of its leadership would not accept the New Testament as containing the binding principles for the church—the *imprint* of the Spirit. The eggshell is gone; it has served its purpose; the nest has its own criteria.

W. B. Blakemore, Disciples of Christ educator, has suggested a new kind of authority in his chapter on church government in Volume III of the Panel of Scholars Reports. The congregation no longer can be the "fundamental unit" of Christianity, whereby the congregation is the only *foundation* for the church.[63] The church, and its order of ministry, must function authoritatively on regional and national levels. "Each level of association is to be understood as the highest authority with respect to those churchly functions which it is peculiarly able to carry out."[64] Restructure operates on this principle. The General Assembly (Council?) "approves general policies and criteria for the order of the ministry," and the Region ordains and "certifies the standing of ministers." The regional ministers act as the regions' "spiritual and administrative leaders" and as the "chief executive officers of the regions."

The Provisional Design calls for "an order of the ministry" separate from the "corporate ministry of God's people." The Order is: "ordained minister, bestowed by ordination"; "licensed minister bestowed by regional license" with an "appropriate act of dedication." The original draft of the *Design* included a third order of ministry—the elder. It was omitted later. The revised *Design* concerning "Ministry" relegated the elder—"him or her"—to that of "local office," along with the "deacon and deaconess." The nineteenth-century concept of threefold ministry has suffered a major reevaluation. Instead of elder, deacon, and evangelist, it has been restructured into area minister (bishop), ordained minister, and licensed minister.

A realignment of the source of authority for the professional ministry has practical effect on the nature of fellowship. The majority of the administrative agency and educational leadership of the Disciples of Christ have endorsed COCU's *Principles of Union.* It is enunciated in the document that only ordained presbyters and bishops can celebrate the

Lord's Supper. Lay leadership can only "assist" or "share" in the service. There is serious doubt as to whether the pastoral ministry of the Disciples of Christ is willing to take this drastic step, further widening the gulf between the clergy and the laity. Certainly the vast majority of the corporate membership would oppose this priestly position.

All segments of the movement seek a ministry that has validity and effectiveness for our times, our people, our mission. The diagnosis has differed, depending on the analysis of present difficulties. The Disciples of Christ have feared a fractionalized, localized ministry. The churches of Christ have fought an intrusion into the authority of the eldership by the evangelists. The Christian churches have sought to breach the provincialism of many of its pastors. The continuity sought by each group varies from jurisdictional, to instructional, to evangelistical, respectively. Which way is forward? The Campbellian plea was for a ministry "duly and scripturally qualified." The plea was at least one of Biblical imperatives.

This was a cry for ministry—service—with the historic Christ of the Scriptures, not the existential Christ of the subconscious. Authority was in the New Testament, not the deliberations of a committee or group. One must ask questions. If Biblical, is the direction "blueprint" or "imprint" of the Spirit? If Biblical, is it complete or only foundation? If Biblical, is it negative or positive, solidified or liquid? If Biblical, is it definitive or explorative? Perhaps what the movement has really said is that apostolic succession is actually a halfway house. The power, the security, the continuity is in our Christocentric service.

Notes to Chapter 4

1. Howard E. Short, *Doctrine and Thought of the Disciples of Christ*, p. 74.

2. A. Campbell, *Christian Baptist*, Vol. II (1824), p. 190.

3. Flavel L. Colley, ed., *Colley-Ketcherside Debate*, p. 118.

4. Z. T. Sweeney, ed., *New Testament Christianity*, Vol. III, p. 57.

5. Flavel L. Colley, ed., *Colley-Ketcherside Debate*, p. 17.

6. J. W. McGarvey, *A Treatise on the Eldership,* p. 18.

7. *Ibid.,* p. 24.

8. J. W. McGarvey, *The Autobiography of J. W. McGarvey* (Lexington: The College of the Bible, 1960, reprint), p. 24.

9. *Lard Quarterly,* Vol. I (September, 1863) (The Old Paths Book Club, reprint), p. 105.

10. *Christian Standard* (May 8, 1869), p. 169.

11. David Edwin Harrell, *Quest For A Christian America,* p. 84.

12. Thomas Munnell, *The Care of All the Churches,* p. 155.

13. *Millennial Harbinger* (January, 1850), p. 22.

14. J. D. Thomas, *We Be Brethren* (Abilene: Biblical Research Press, 1958), p. 146.

15. H. Leo Boles, *The Eldership of the Churches of Christ* (Nashville: Gospel Advocate Co., n.d.), p. 32.

16. *Apostolic Review* (November 10, 1913), p. 16.

17. Thomas Munnell, *The Care of All the Churches,* p. 41.

18. *Ibid.,* p. 272.

19. *Apostolic Times* (April 15, 1869), p. 4.

20. Edgar J. Goodspeed, *The Apostolic Fathers* (New York: Harper & Bros., 1950), p. 208.

21. *Ibid.,* p. 230.

22. T. M. Lindsay, *The Church and the Ministry in the Early Centuries* (London: Hodder & Stoughton, Ltd., n.d.), p. 205.

23. William Mander, "The Ministry," *Toward Christian Union,* James Gray, ed. (Leicester, Union Committee of Churches of Christ, 1960), p. 38.

24. Carroll C. Cotten, *The Imperative Is Leadership* (St. Louis: Bethany Press, 1973), p. 19.

25. *Ibid.,* p. 19.

26. *Ibid.,* p. 30.

27. *Ibid.,* pp. 30, 31.

28. *Ibid.,* p. 22.

29. Ronald E. Osborn, *In Christ's Place,* p. 257.

30. *The Revival of the Churches,* Vol. III, p. 186.

31. "Pulpit, Parson and Pew," *The Christian* (January 24, 1965), p. 6.

32. *Ibid.,* p. 7.

33. W. E. Garrison, *Whence and Whither the Disciples of Christ* (St. Louis: Christian Board of Publication, 1954), p. 93.

34. Z. T. Sweeney, ed., *New Testament Christianity,* Vol. I (Columbus, Indiana: printed for editor, 1923), p. 445.

35. W. R. Walker, *A Ministering Ministry* (Cincinnati: Standard Publishing, 1938), p. 31.

36. *Ibid.,* p. 120.

37. *Ibid.,* cf. pp. 184, 185.

38. W. T. Moore, *Living Pulpit,* pp. 39, 40.

39. J. W. McGarvey, *A Treatise on the Eldership,* p. 65.

40. Louise King, *Memoirs of David King* (reprint), p. 289.

41. F. D. Kershner, *The Restoration Handbook,* Series III, p. 12.

42. "Key Man," *Christian Standard* (September 26, 1971), pp. 17, 18.

43. "Rethinking the Term Pastor," *Christian Standard* (September 9, 1961), p. 573.

44. "The Ministry Does Not Stand Alone," Address, Kansas City: International Convention of Christian Churches (Disciples of Christ), 1961.

45. *Christian Standard* (July 16, 1972), p. 5.

46. Carroll C. Cotten, *The Imperative Is Leadership,* pp. 35-37.

47. James D. Murch, *The Free Church,* p. 80.

48. *Millennial Harbinger* (October, 1835), extra, p. 496.

49. *Millennial Harbinger* (May, 1837), p. 231. See Campbell's reply to James Otey in *Ibid.,* (July, 1835), p. 293. Also *Ibid.,* (August, 1849), p. 460.

50. Isaac Errett, *The Querists' Drawer,* cf. p. 17; See W. R. Walker, *A Ministering Ministry,* p. 99.

51. A. S. Johnson, *The Holy Spirit and the Human Mind (Knoxville: Grant-Ogden Co., 1903), p. 95.*

52. *Report of the Commission on the Ministry* (British Churches of Christ, Birmingham, England: Berian Press, 1947), p. 9.

53. Thomas Munnell, *The Care of All the Churches,* p. 122.

54. *Ibid.,* p. 125.

55. James D. Murch, *Christian Minister's Manual,* p. 153.

56. J. Rogers, *Biography of Eld. Barton Warren Stone,* as reported on p. 185.

57. W. Scott, *The Messiah, or Great Demonstration* (Cincinnati: H. S. Bosworth, 1859), p. 138.

58. T. Stringfellow, "The Episcopacy," *Millennial Harbinger* (May, 1845), p. 207.

59. Hans Kung, *Why Priests?* (New York: Doubleday & Co., 1972), p. 44.

60. *Millennial Harbinger* (1835), p. 292.

61. C. C. Morrison, *The Unfinished Reformation* (New York: Harper & Bros. Publishers, 1953), p. 164.

62. "The Council and the Church—A New Look," an address by Stephen J. England, July 28, 1966, p. 9.

63. "The Issue of Polity For Disciples Today," *The Revival of the Churches,* Vol. III, p. 67.

64. *Ibid.,* pp. 75, 76.

5

the call and its confirmation

The Call

Rejecting the Supernatural

The *Last Will and Testament of the Springfield Presbytery* stressed the importance of "candidates for the Gospel Ministry" to "obtain license from God to preach the simple Gospel, *with the Holy Ghost sent down from Heaven.*" None should assume the "honour" of preaching "but he that is called of God, as was Aaron." Barton W. Stone does not elaborate on what he means by the phrase "as was Aaron." Presumably it was as a spokesman for God and not as a priest. Perhaps Exodus 4:15, 16 was in his mind: "And I will be with thy [Moses'] mouth; and with his mouth, and will teach you what ye shall do. And he shall be thy spokesman unto the people." This reference to Aaron was immediately followed by, "We *will,* that the church of Christ resume her native right of internal government—try her candidates for the ministry as to their soundness in the faith, acquaintance with experimental religion, gravity and aptness to teach."

In 1827 Stone called attention to "many and great improprieties" in the preaching ministry because some "are impressed with the belief that they are called to preach the gospel." Evidently many were feeling the call of the Spirit and striking out as evangelists. Stone was insistent about receiving prior approval before preaching, and saw support in 2 Corinthians 3:1 and Acts 13:1, 4.

> We view it an impropriety for a person, impressed with the idea that he is divinely called to preach, to go abroad and travel from country to country preaching without being sent by the churches with letters of recommendation.[1]

To Stone, there was no mysterious call apart from the approval and recommendation of at least one congregation. A man's awareness of God's hand upon him was his call, which was fulfilled and completed at his ordination, being the confirmation of this call. Stone made less of an issue of this in his writings than did Alexander Campbell, yet he had been personally troubled more. As a young man Stone wanted to enter the ministry but was unable to experience a "soul-shaking call." David Caldwell convinced him that such was not essential.

Objective standards of selection appear in Acts 6:1-6—good reputation, Spirit activated, wise and discerning. There is no hint of a subjective, secret call. Ronald Osborn states, "Aside from Saul's conversion, and call to the apostolate, Scripture gives no instance in which any one received a private call from God to the public ministry of the church."[2]

Reasoning by Lockean epistomology of sensationalism, Campbell concluded that "nothing short of divine attestations or miracles can evince that any man is especially called of the Spirit of God to instruct us in the Christian religion."[3] Inasmuch as the Scriptures were adequate revelation, it was foolish for any man to claim to be "called and sent of God." If there be no new divine message from the skies, there is no need for a divine messenger or new prophet. Campbell was caustic against this "pretense of a divine call" for he believed it provided a major avenue for clergy lording it over the people of God.[4] Requiring the people to depend upon a "priesthood" interpretation of the Bible violated its nature as an intelligible book open to exposition by any capable disciple. With the "pretense of a divine call" it was an easy step for the divines to seek a "confederation of themselves into associated bodies, called councils, synods, general assemblies, associations or conferences."[5] William West feels that this argument over "ministerial calling" was one of Campbell's major breaks with Calvinism.[6]

The idea of accompanying "holy grace" when a man got his "call" was folly to Campbell. A man's credentials were his character, talents, and inclinations to help others in the name of the Lord. "The same call which the rich man has to relieve the poor when he discovers them, is that which an intelligent Christian has to instruct those ignorant of God."[7] The "hireling" claims a call, then sets out to learn his "trade." The Christian bishop is called by the brethren, because he has the qualifications *already*.[8] But there is no completed call until a congregation decides the candidate is eligible to represent Christ. No man is competent to decide finally for himself.[9]

In the nineteenth century the Disciples accepted the dogma that a supernatural call was irrational and unscriptural. But the expressions were so arbitrary that W. T. Moore warned in 1907 that extreme rationalism had produced "a reaction which has well-nigh proved fatal to the ministry itself."

> From the notion that "sights and sounds" were necessary to an assurance of fitness for the ministry, the prevailing rationalism has practically carried the public mind to the opposite extreme where the divine element is completely eliminated.[10]

Nature of the Call

The phrase "call to the ministry" is real even though it may be ambiguous and possessed of countless tangential interpretations. Concern regarding the call has not been abstract. There has rarely been a time when the brotherhood did not need ministers. Every decade seemed to have its cries for workers to tend to the harvest. In 1839 Alexander Campbell answered in the *Harbinger* a cry for help for more "preachers and pastors to take care of the numerous flocks we already have." He said, "We want a thousand evangelists."[11] As early as 1850 the Kentucky Christian Missionary Society passed a resolution for the enlistment of young men for the ministry. Similar efforts were made for Missouri and Ohio a few years later. The leadership wanted men to answer the call to service. What would persuade them? What kind of man should be persuaded? What constitutes a godly desire to serve?

C. L. Loos, one of the scholarly teachers of the middle nineteenth century, was leery of the professional clergyman. He said, "Where grace is a mere scholastic term and piety a formalism," then "clergymen are still manufactured." But "preachers of the gospel are not made in this same, easy, off-hand way."[12] These aspects of a call are summed up succinctly by T. P. Haley:

> The desire to preach without the ability is not the call; the desire and the ability without the opportunity is not the call; but ability, desire and opportunity may be taken as the divine call.[13]

God calls the capable. God calls the capable through the rational processes. A call is not just a feeling or an emotion, though, like a conversion, it may take more than one form. It may be a gradual awareness of a task to be done, or it may come more forcefully in a climactic synthesis of comprehension, volition, and emotion. There is the thrust of God calling. It has a supernatural origin, if not a supernatural expression. W. T. Moore suggested some determining marks as guides for a call, though recognizing that such a holy and individual thing defies regimentation. He believed one should examine himself for a "reasonable amount of native intellectual force" to preach effectively, possess the highest "moral qualifications," be in good physical condition, and display an "irresistible conviction of duty."[14] It is instructive that Alexander Campbell in 1811 in determining whether or not to be ordained, listed "the providential dispensations" he had experienced and which he considered to "bind me under obligation to be specially devoted to Him." Campbell listed twelve items, and Number XI was "In giving me a call from the Church to preach the Gospel."[15]

W. R. Walker, in his 1938 volume, *A Ministering Ministry*, was concerned with the "call." He was not convinced that "denying oneself" was a sufficient motivation. "The ascetic abstainer is not the type approved by Christ. Such a one may be indulging 'self' by his very austerity."[16] To be God's choice a man must have ability. Walker meant "everything that goes into the making up of the man—intellectuality, spirituality, devotion, willingness to endure hardship, etc. One thus endowed may be certain of his 'call.' "[17]

As with Isaiah (chapter 6) one does not lightly receive the vision of the uplifted God. C. B. Tupper in *Called–In Honor* would question the validity of a call if the recipient accepted it "without a sense of profound personal unworthiness and inadequacy."[18] And Hampton Adams believed that one must attach the "moral equivalent of war" to the call of the self-giving ministry of the church.[19] A few years later Adams saw the need of qualifications beyond a love for people and devotion to the church. He suggested certain "personal aptitudes" necessary for a successful ministry: delight in continued study, capacity for public speaking, a willingness for teamwork, aptness in counseling, and possessing administrative ability.[20]

In 1954 the Disciples of Christ commissioned twenty-eight study groups around the nation to prepare statements on the ministry for the 1955 World Convention of Churches of Christ. The Nashville group asserted that a call's genuineness "must be tested by the resources which one is willing to devote and consecrate to this high calling." One who feels the call must ever keep in mind those "high qualities of Christian character, mental alertness and capacity for leadership which not only give proof of his call but qualify him to be chosen by the church."

Hollis Lee Turley in an address before the 1961 International Convention expressed the rising frustrations and lack of security in many of the Disciples of Christ ministers. One solution was the need for "a resurgence of the feeling that God calls men into the ministry. Men who feel that they have been called of God to a great task will not easily become discouraged even in the midst of frustration." The great Old Testament prophets were able to survive only because their call "had its origin in an act of God." These prophets "did not answer the call of duty or conscience, the call of community or of country; they responded to the call of God." Unfortunately there is a rising percentage of current Disciples of Christ ministers who have abandoned the older concept of a "life calling," for allegiance to a vocation, or a succession of vocations, as the clergyman seeks meaning for his life. This attitude seems reflected in D. Ray Lindley's volume *Apostle of Freedom.*

> The call to the ministry consisted neither in a personal ambition on the part of the one called nor a mandate from the Holy Spirit, but in a social contract with the church. . . . The office of the ministry was in the nature of a social relationship, and call, appointment, and ordination were all integral to a social contract with the congregation.[21]

Traditionally the Disciples have rejected the interpretation that a "call from God" is a unilateral decision of an individual. Christ instituted the church, and through this body calls His ministry. The call is a contract with the church, but on a deeper level than a "social contract"—rather a soul contract. The church challenges through all its services and gifts. This mutuality between an individual and the church is not without intelligent signs or guideposts. God is calling when through one's association with the church he has a recurring sense of "oughtness" for ministry, when this sense is increasingly personal, when one has a growing awareness that the answer to the world's problems is primarily spiritual, and when efforts of service give an expanding sense of Christian satisfaction. A quarter of a century ago W. W. Wasson summed it up by the phrase, "the desire to live and to promote the highest life possible."[22]

In *The Free Church* J. D. Murch strikes a note of independency and individuality. He recognizes that "under normal circumstances" a local church is "used of God to prepare and ordain men for the ministry." However, when a man is "convinced that 'necessity is laid' on him" and he must preach the gospel, "all the church councils; elders, college professors, secretaries, and bishops in the world cannot prevent him."[23]

Influences Affecting a Call

The Disciples refused to consider a call in terms of God's supernatural, perhaps magical, intervention of grace. Throughout the nineteenth century there were repeated pleas in the journals for preachers, and the preachers, evangelists, and pastors lent their voices in proclaiming the need. However, the Disciples came into the twentieth century before they began seriously to study the natural forces that exert telling influences on decisions for the ministry.

In 1952 Harlie L. Smith, president of the Board of Higher Education of the Disciples of Christ, sent questionnaires to men in ten graduate seminaries. Of those returned, 477 were usable in the tabulation. One important fact which needs further evaluation was that, excluding the ministry, very few students had fathers who were professional men.[24] One wonders what aspects of the home life of a professional man are not conducive to ministerial tendencies. However, the ministry did not acquit itself much better. Only 11 percent of Disciples of Christ graduate students, according to the Smith study, had been reared in a parsonage. This is somewhat less than the percentage of father-son continuation in other professions. Other studies in the 1950's and 1960's indicate that the brotherhood draws its ministerial candidates largely from the middle class and lower income families. It is estimated that only 50 percent decide upon the ministry before graduating from high school.[25] This seems to be a surprisingly low percentage, considering the efforts made by the churches for commitment in camps and conferences. It probably is higher among the churches of Christ and Christian churches. There also appears to be a differing ratio as to the number of students who complete a course of study for the ministry and enter the field, between the Disciples of Christ and the other two segments. W. A. Welch, president of Lexington Theological Seminary (formerly College of the Bible), expresses concern over the high "attrition-rate." He estimates that "it takes about eight high school 'Timothies' to produce a single 'Paul,' fully prepared and active in ministry five years after seminary."[26]

The impact, for all aspects of the brotherhood, is that there must be steady, active, widespread recruitment for full-time Christian vocations, if there is to be a sufficient number of ministers to move the churches forward. The first recommendation of the 1973 Disciples Study Commission on Ministerial Education is "the development of an educated, talented, and culturally diverse professional ministry."[27] This sounds a different note from goals expressed by a 1973 editorial in the *Christian Standard.* Here Edwin Hayden expressed the purpose of ministry was to be "evangelistic," "edifying," and to give men an "equipping ministry, assisting Christians in preparation for service."[28] One chooses a leader in accordance with the kind of service he will render and the tasks he must do and the stress he must endure. The criteria for the call will be different between a clergyman and a preacher, an "enabler" and a pastor, a servant and a professional.

The Smith study, the Welsh analysis, and other evaluations all agree that the strongest influence for commitment is the local pastor. The order of positive factors appears to be: pastor, mother, youth camp or conference, other ministers, father, local youth group. The decline of ministerial students by 20 percent in the past ten years for the Disciples of Christ cannot but reflect the fact that more than one thousand Disciples congregations were without a full-time pastor in 1972, in accordance with the *Year Book.* Earl Waldrop, vice-chancellor of Texas Christian University, experienced a different order of influence. "More young men have gone into the ministry through young people's conferences than from any other source." He does agree that the local minister is the single most important individual to challenge young men to be ministers. He should be "on constant lookout for the best, the brightest, the strongest young men in his congregation."[29] Often overlooked, says Waldrop, is the "definite obligation" of parents to "hold up the chirch with their loyalty and support."[30] P. H. Welshimer had this to say to parents nearly a half century ago:

If you desire your boy to preach, put religious papers on the table for him to read. Speak well of the ministry and treat your preacher in a way that will commend the ministry to your son. . . . Many a boy who had capabilities has had his mind turned from the ministry by the treatment his home preacher received at the hands of the church.[31]

The recognized conflict of aim and purpose between the Disciples clergymen and the membership may in part stem from the fact that only 8.5 percent of the "professional ministerial" groups "ranked meeting spiritual and religious needs of the congregation as of first importance, while an average of 23.3 percent of the laity groups ranked meeting these needs as primary."[32] Inasmuch as the educated minister commands a salary of several thousand dollars less than his counterpart in the other professions, the youth to whom a call is presented needs to see spiritual satisfactions and compensations. If the local pastor does not reflect this spirituality, he substantially reduces the inducements necessary to elicit a response. The fact is, the image of ministry reflected usually begets its kind, if it is not too sterile for any conception. Robert Burns, when minister of the Peachtree Christian Church, Atlanta, Georgia, discovered that lack of information to the youth was a major oversight. His experience with those "who have seriously considered" the ministry was that "83.5 percent say they do not enlist because no person, no organization, no pastor, no parent expressed the desire for them to do so."[33]

Some in all segments of the movement would still agree

with the editor of the 1904 *Illinois Christian News,* who disapproved of having young men "solicited and urged" to "become preachers." To him, the "spirit of the church" will add the "proper numbers." The true church had no room for half-hearted, half-souled men in the ministry.[34] However, most observers have not seen a correlation between planned campaigning and solicitation and the result of unqualified ministers. Perhaps C. L. Loos expressed the shepherd heart of the Savior when he wrote in 1865:

> We must seek for them diligently, as for anything precious; and when found by all means that the Holy Spirit places in our hands develop them for their glorious task. How many such valuable, true hearts have been lost to the evangelical work by the careless, cold indifference of the church.[35]

E. K. Higdon, at one time director of missionary training for the United Christian Missionary Society, called for more comprehensive testing of candidates in order to exclude certain psychological types. He would extend the testing to all seminaries, and not reserve it for the Foreign Division of the Society. Higdon indicated that "a rather large percentage of homosexuals" seek the ministry. In the United States where "it is estimated that 37 percent of adult males suffer from this illness," the brotherhood should "adopt methods of discovering them among the volunteers and of disqualifying them from all Christian ministries."[36] Higdon believed that the Foreign Division's successful work with missionaries was adequate proof of the practicality of rigorous examinations. He documented that of the 120 missionaries sent abroad in the 1943-1953 period, only three who received "good" to "excellent" on psychiatric testing failed to make satisfactory adjustments.[37]

Objective tests undoubtedly are important in outlining psychological problems, but they have limitations for the broad field of public ministry. Present-day psychiatry would have difficulty evaluating a "called of God" candidate. The call is not reducible to psychological standards or physical fitness. History has proven that the possession of the Spirit can outweigh a multitude of "sins" of failure in examinations. The voice of the church should have substantial force in ascertaining the validity of a call. It may not always be the voice of God, but it is usually a helpful indication. The church must also keep in mind that the Spirit sometimes works in peculiar ways and channels. The power is not invalidated when the church fails to acknowledge, but the opportunity becomes severely limited.

In spite of the persuasive arguments by the Study Commission on Ministerial Education of the Disciples of Christ, F. E. Smith, former secretary for the Pension Fund, represents the major thinking of the brotherhood by his declaration more than thirty years ago: "The ministry is not a profession. . . . God is the first to act with respect to men entering the ministry. Before every man lay hands on in ordination, . . . God has put His finger on His man and called him into His service."[38]

Ordination

Resolution #49 passed by the General Assembly of the Disciples of Christ in Louisville in 1971 called for Regions to certify the standing of clergymen in their Region, excepting chaplains and missionaries. These two latter groups are certified by a special committee of the General Board. The criteria for certification by the Region included: faithful performance of the duties of a minister, participation in programs of study, research, growth and renewal, and maintaining relationship with the Disciples of Christ. J. J. Van Boskirk, regional minister of the Capital Area, does not view these restrictions as guidelines to "be used, by 'agency people' to 'whip into line' someone."[39] He sees it as the first opportunity clergymen have had in getting "a real say in the ordering of their profession."[40] Van Boskirk views it as the culmination of twenty-five years of rebelling against the tyranny of local congregations ordaining whomever they chose as long as he showed promise and was of upright character.

The Restructured Disciples of Christ use the phrase in their recent publications, "certification and ordination." This refers to "processes of ordination and induction into ministerial standing of the church *following completion of formal education*" (emphasis mine).[41] For the first time in Disciples history the Disciples of Christ are attempting to parallel the concept of ordination with the admission to practice in the legal and medical professions. The movement began with ordination as the church's response to the individual's expression of a call. There is, however, one parallelism in this new approach to Alexander Campbell's view of elder-ordination. That ordination was a setting aside and a recognition of talents already developed. In Campbell's case it was recognition of spiritual maturity. In the Disciples of Christ it is recognition of educational attainment. But this is exactly the concept of professional ministry that Campbell abhored. The Disciples of Christ seem to have gone full circle in 160 years.

Nineteenth-Century Views

Thomas Campbell and Barton Stone had a high appreciation of ordination and Alexander Campbell considered it "his duty to be ordained" in 1812. His ordination certificate submitted to the court was signed: "Thomas Campbell, Senior Minister of the First Church of the Christian Association of Washington."[42] Alexander saw ordination as important as a social and moral compact with the church.

In the *Christian Messenger,* Vol. I, May 25, 1827, Stone was recounting the "History of the Christian Church in the West." He discussed his understanding of ordination.

> When the church is satisfied, they manifest it by ordaining him. In all this, the church confers no power, human or divine; but only the privilege of exercising the power and authority, which they believe he has received from God, in that particular society. This privilege, the church may recall, the candidate may forfeit or voluntarily resign. But neither the refusal of the church, his own forfeiture or resignation of that particular privilege, can disannul the original call of God, or the obligation of the candidate to obey.

Ordination here is the privilege of function in a particular religious society. There is no hint of sacramentalism, nor of life-long status. The "laying on of hands" that accompanied the rite conveyed no "spiritual gifts." To Campbell and Stone ordination was meaningful as it represented the formal support of the people, a public testimony and recognition of the present capacity of the candidate.[43]

The oldest extant ordination certificate in the archives of the *Historical Society* is for 1809. It reads:

We the underwritten do certify that according to a previous appointment on east fork of little Barren on Monday after the third Sabbath of July 1809 Samuel Boyd was publicly set apart by ordination for the work of the Gospel Ministry according to the manner of the Christian Church then present at that place—and that as such he is received by the different branches of sd. church and in full communion and good standing. Given under our hands the day and year above mentioned.   *Benjamin Lyn,*
Lewis Bynam[44]

Some early nineteenth-century certificates mention "prayer and the imposition of hands" and "fasting and prayer and the imposition of hand." However, it seems certain that fasting usually accompanied ordination in the early decades of the movement.

Records mentioning ordination are not as plentiful as desirable for the period up to 1840, but there was appreciation for it in many quarters. Here are some examples. William Hayden was ordained in October, 1828, by Walter Scott and Adamson Bentley, after he had been chosen as the evangelistic associate of Scott.[45] Michael Combs, converted around 1822 by David Purviance, was ordained later by Jesse Frazier.[46] Converted by Peter Ainslie in 1827, John Curtis was ordained to the ministry in 1830.[47] Beverly Vawter left the Baptist church, was rebaptized and then ordained in 1819 by Elders J. Crafton and John Henderson. C. L. Loos was ordained by Alexander Campbell and Robert Richardson in 1849.[48]

In his *Scheme of Redemption,* Milligan took a more pragmatic turn. "The Common sense of mankind requires" that candidates for the ministry "shall be installed with some solemn and impressive ceremonies."[49] He referred to Acts 6:5, 6; 13:1-3; 14:23; 1 Timothy 4:14 to show a pattern. The reasonable man would draw the conclusion that "all the Deacons, Elders, and Evangelists of the primitive Church were ordained by the imposition of hands, with prayer and fasting." The binding effect is such that no one can "be legally and properly set apart as an officer or minister of the Christian Church without these solemnities."[50]

However, many of the nineteenth-century leaders did not follow the logic of Milligan. James Shannon was one. He wrote several articles in the 1839 *Millennial Harbinger,* and engaged in a pen debate with Thomas Campbell in the December issue. Campbell sided with his son Alexander. Shannon stated that there was "not a single passage in the New Testament which records the fact that any disciple ever had hands laid on him to authorize him to preach the gospel and baptize believers."

Shannon had sought ordination about 1822 in the Presbyterian ministry after arriving in America from Ireland. Upon becoming convinced that infant baptism was wrong, he refused the ordination, was immersed, and joined the Baptist church.[51] Shannon later accepted the Disciples position, and during his career as an educator was president of five colleges. In 1839, while president of the College of Louisiana he wrote that preaching the gospel was a moral duty and did not require ordination as a prerequisite. Later, such a prominent Disciple as J. H. Garrison was never ordained. His son, W. E. Garrison, was not ordained "until middle life," after his "name had been in the list of ministers in the Disciples Yearbook for more than twenty years."[52]

David Lipscomb also refused ordination. His personality combined independence to the point of stubbornness and natural timidity. He said, "I started out to preach believing preachers were appointed by laying on of hands. I failed to submit to it, because I did not care to be considered a preacher."[53] This approach probably came from Tolbert Fanning, Lipscomb's teacher and associate in many enterprises. This feeling is current today among the churches of Christ. B. C. Goodpasture, a leading editor, was of the opinion that at the middle of the twentieth century there were still few advocates of formal ordination, the concept being that when God calls, man will preach. In discussing preachers who did not have the "right spirit," James D. Bales wrote in 1967: "Since we do not have the authority to issue or to revoke 'licenses' to preach there is no way that we can keep them from preaching."[54] His solution was for the elders to "dispense with his services" if the preacher did not reform.

Thomas Campbell knew that ordination had value for the church, and was a needed protection. In a postscript to a lengthy letter in Volume 7 of the *Christian Baptist,* he alluded to Alexander's proposed "series of sermons to young preachers," and posed several questions about qualifications for the ministry. The last two were:

6. Should he be an approved member of a christian church, and have its approbation, both as to his age, and talents; as a person of considerable standing, of established character, of sound comprehensive scriptural knowledge, duly acquainted with the actual condition and character of the religious world?

7. Or may every person whose zeal, or self-conceit may prompt him, become a prophet, without any respect to the qualifications above specified, or any qualifications at all; and say what he pleases in the name of the Lord, without respect to any authority divine or human? And have the churches of the saints no cognizance of such characters—no defense against them?[55]

Alexander Campbell, like most of us, found theories conflicting in their practical application. This is evident in his concepts of the nature of the church, and the assumptions of the uneducated "babes in Christ." Campbell declared on many occasions, "An individual church or congregation of Christ's disciples is the only ecclesiastical body recognized in the New Testament." It would logically follow that any local congregation should ordain to the "gospel ministry." However, Campbell also had a fear of uneducated opinions. Freedom in the church had its checkpoints against the "common ignoramuses which constitute the majority." Ordaining bishops did not have the same import as ordaining preachers for the brotherhood. He illustrated this with a hypothetical church of thirty members, ten males and twenty females, and of them only about four of the men had "plain common sense." They decide that one of the men should be "commissioned" to preach the gospel.

Now the question is, Are they to be condemned or justified who consider this man legitimately introduced into the world as a teacher of religion? Is any other society bound to credit his pretensions, or to receive him *bona fide* as a legally authorized teacher of the christian religion, and ruler in the christian church?[56]

Unfortunately Campbell did not answer his own question. It was enough for him to illustrate this extreme tendency in some religious groups, this "most licentious equality, which recognized neither the letter nor the spirit of subordination."[57]

Barton Stone also viewed with alarm the concept of such congregational independence that each group felt itself obligated to propagate the ministry. He viewed the right of ordination as a privilege of the ministry itself. W. E. Garrison observed:

> Stone criticized those who thought that a church could "induct into the ministerial office," he considered that a function as belonging to the "bishops and elders." If a minister is charged with "preaching doctrine contrary to the gospel," he should be examined by a "conference of bishops and elders."[58]

The influence of Stone is seen in the procedure of the Christian Connexion and the role their conferences played. Professor Millard wrote in 1847: "At such conferences candidates for the ministry are examined, received and commended."[59] Previously the 1825 report from the General Conference of the United States had recommended:

> Agreed, that in case of ordination, we deem it expedient that the candidate have the approbation of a church or churches, with the council of at least three Elders, and for the ordination of a deacon, the advice of one Elder.[60]

Both Campbell and Stone agreed to this principle: first, approval by the church and then ordination. They differed as to the extent of the approval necessary, and the persons involved in the actual ceremony. The majority of the churches followed Campbell's position of the propriety of the local eldership laying on of hands. Campbell believed that if an evangelist was present he should have priority in the action, but such was not necessary.[61] W. K. Pendleton believed that when ordination was neglected the "office ceases to be regarded as a gift of the church" and can be violated as a kind of "free public domain" by any "squatter" who may enter for temporary employment or profit."[62]

Twentieth-Century Views

As the frontier began to fade, and with it the bold individualism, the practice of ordination became more prevalent.

The Commission on Ordination reported to the 1939 International Convention that "85 percent of our ministers have been ordained and that with the younger men the percentage probably runs as high as 95 percent or 98 percent."[63] Attempts were made early to control ordination and not leave it as the possession of each local congregation. The 1857 Constitution of the North Carolina Conference implied area control. This position was attacked on many occasions in *American Christian Review*. J. T. Walsh, an official of the conference, remarked about the practice of examining ministerial candidates that formally began in 1872: "We do not claim for conventions that they always do right, but we do say that local congregations err and do wrong, just as often, and we think more frequently."[64]

Slowly the Disciples of Christ moved to the position that ordination should no longer be the "one service concern" of one congregation. The feeling was that no one congregation had the right to instigate an action that the brotherhood may suffer from, without assuming the responsibility of controlling that action. During the 1937 International Convention a resolution, included in the report of the Commission on Ordination, suggested that a candidate's "ordination should be publicly recognized at the next state convention" and that the next "annual Year Book" should carry "not only the name of the newly ordained minister with the date of his ordination but the names of the sponsoring ministers, as well."[65] The purpose at this stage of development was to give a sense of catholicity and avoid the dangers of sacerdotalism and clericalism.

The Disciples of Christ have shown a growing tendency in the past thirty years to consult the State Secretary (now area minister) when planning an ordination. C. E. Lemmon could say in the *Reformation of Tradition* some ten years ago: "In the past twenty years in Missouri it has been unusual for a minister to be ordained without the presence and participation of the state secretary."[66]

The 1940 Richmond convention in Indiana proposed a Plan of Ordination. Opposition came in a deluge. In May, 1940, some sixty Indiana ministers met and recorded opposition to the plan, seeing it as a violation of "the local church as an autonomous and free church." The suggestion in the plan that three local churches participate in the ceremony was countered with, "This is purely and simply the calling of a presbytery." An editorial in the *Christian Standard* said the commission was an "approach to ecclesiasticism" and a "threat to the freedom of the churches."[67] The editorial staff of the *Standard* denounced the 1940 plan for two main reasons that would also apply to the present Disciples of Christ procedures. One, it sets up arbitrary standards of education; two, it specifically excluded theological questions from those propounded to the candidate.

Dean E. Walker, then a professor at the College of Religion, Butler University (Christian Theological Seminary), objected to the regimentation and lack of voluntariness. Frank H. Marshall, dean of the College of the Bible, Phillips University, acknowledged the seriousness of the problem of ordination and the lack of maturity and experience that many displayed at ordination. Because it "invests the candidate with the full and final approval and authority of the church," it should be carefully considered.

> In my judgment such ordination ought to be deferred until the Candidate has really prepared himself for his life work. Certainly, the completion of his usual college curriculum, and, if possible additional seminary training."[68]

Marshall and Joe Belcastro recognized the need for "higher standards for ordination," but did not want to subject the congregations to "an external power" that would "develop into a hierarchy."[69]

Three years later an editorial in the *Standard* said the "church surrenders its heritage" when the congregation abdicates ordination and "control of the ministry" to the state organization. The idea being criticized was that "ordination by state committees is much easier, and seemingly more 'practical' than for each congregation through its elders to study the doctrine and protect itself from unworthy preachers."[70] James D. Murch represented the broad conservative view when he wrote in the *Christian Minister's Manual*, "Any local church has the right of ordination."[71] The responsibility lay with the elders to investigate the background, reputation, and deportment. If such a report was favorable "the applicant should be examined by the eldership as to his knowledge of the Word of God, his view of Christian doctrine, his call to the ministry, and his further fitness for the office."[72] Murch added, though the local eldership would preside at the installation, "neighboring ministers may be invited to participate."[73] This concept of inter-congregational participation has not had as widespread usage among the Christian churches as it should. When it has been used, rarely have the eldership of two or more congregations jointly made initial inquiries of fitness. Ordination, until recently in certain circles, was never understood as a sacred investiture. It carried no monopoly for divine grace. When performed by the laying on of hands and intercessory prayer, it was the church's recognition of God's call upon an individual to take public leadership. Authority is given, not special powers.

Campbell understood ordination as a corporate acknowledgement of one as a public minister, for life. "The whole community chooses—the seniors ordain. *This is the apostolic tradition. . . . It is immutable.*"[74] J. W. McGarvey agreed: "The only certain fact is that the people elected their officers."[75] The New Testament gave Campbell and others proof of their position. In the selection of Matthias (Acts 1:21-26) the entire company nominated two men who qualified. In Acts 6:5, 6, the seven were elected by "the whole multitude," and then the apostles "laid their hands on them." Again, according to Acts 15:22-25, after the Jerusalem conference "the apostles and elders, with the whole church" selected and commissioned the representatives to Antioch. Beyond local action, there was church-wide recognition. Letters of "commendation" were carried on the journeys. See 2 Corinthians 4:2; 5:12; 6:4.

Campbell's concept has relevancy today only for elders, deacons, and deaconesses, not for the professional ministry. There is a congregational vote when a minister of the Christian churches or Disciples of Christ is "called" to labor in a pastorate, but rarely as a response to his original call into full-time service. In the churches of Christ the membership does not actually call an evangelist to preach. They are advised of the decision of the eldership and customarily give informal approval.

James M. Moudy, chancellor of Texas Christian University,

has stressed the leadership aspect of ordination, seeing it as more vital than commencement to ministry.

> The expectation of ordination is not of ministry, but of leadership! All are ministers, but not all are leaders.
> Herein lies one of the greatest weaknesses of those who ordain men to the public ministry. They pay too little attention to potentiality of leadership.[76]

There is no necessity to bifurcate public ministry and leadership, for they intertwine. The damage in recruitment has more often occurred where ministry has been looked upon as officious more than as effective; as position rather than as function.

William J. Moore takes a position similar to that taken by James Challen in the 1830's. Moore maintains, "There is no specific reference to ordination in the New Testament. In some instances where people assumed leadership the 'laying on of hands' took place, but there is nothing to support the view that this was the universal practice when people took office."[77]

Herald B. Monroe, General Secretary of Ohio Society of Christian Churches (Disciples), sees more importance in ordination than William Moore. "The ordination vow makes for the difference between laymen and the ministers, and is, a holy office created by God, and not a purely sociological phenomenon."[78] Monroe represents the view of most clergymen today in the Disciples of Christ. The ministry now has taken on as much ecclesiastical meaning as it formerly did functional.

In *A Response to Lund* in 1952, the Faith and Order Committee of the Disciples of Christ stated that the minister is the "preacher and the leader of worship, but strictly speaking he exercises under appointment a representative priestly *function* rather than holding a priestly *office* or standing in a priestly *order.* . . . For this reason Disciples have traditionally avoided the terms 'clergy' and 'laity.' The ordination of a minister is a public act of consecration to his task."[79] The theology of this *Response* is no longer representative of the views of Regional and General ministers of the Disciples of Christ. More and more the theology of this segment implies that authority rests in the ministry itself, not just its message.

A. T. DeGroot, noted historian, says this leadership has fostered "the Siamese twins" of Restructure and COCU on the Disciples of Christ. He warns that COCU would require that "all Disciples ministers must be reordained in the apostolic succession."[80]

In the British churches of Christ the full-time minister is ordained by the conference, which is an annual affair, not "delegated," but composed of individual church members. The laying on of hands at a special session of the conference signifies ordination by the whole church. Locally ordained elders and deacons have continued to be regarded as part of the church's ministry, even though maintaining secular employment. The conference set up a Commission on Ordination in 1936, and it gave its report in 1942. William Mander observed:

> Special emphasis is laid on the matter of the ordination of those to whom the call of God had come and who were fitted by the requisite gifts for office in the Church. Particular note is made of the fact that "it is Christ Himself, through the Church, who appoints, ordains and sends His Ministers forth."[81]

The British do not require one to be ordained in order to officiate at the ordinances. In the conference report concerning the 1937 Faith and Order study at Edinburg, James Gray said:

> We are amongst those who hold that ordination is not an essential condition to the validity of the sacraments provided that the Church appoints the minister of the sacraments. . . . We agree with the Archbishop of York (Dr. William Temple) who says: "What is conferred in ordination is not *power* to make sacramental a rite which otherwise would not be such, but *authority (potestas)* to administer sacraments which belong to the Church, and which, therefore, can only be rightly administered by those who hold the Church's commission to do so."[82]

Ministers are people of authority, but they are also under authority of the Word. The message is their power. They have no authority apart from it. Ordination should be neither the exclusive possession of each separate congregation, nor the act of a hierarchy or a supra-congregational leader. Ordination is at once local and general, personal and professional, existential and futuristic. Ordination is not just a convenience. It is the people's proclamation to the validity of the call. It is the minister's challenge and the church's defense against those not worthy of His cross.

Licensing

Thomas Campbell and Barton Stone were licensed before being ordained to the Presbyterian ministry. Alexander Campbell was licensed by the Brush Run congregation prior to his ordination.[83] However, the theory of licensing that was held by the Presbyterians was not carried over into the Disciples in the nineteenth and early twentieth centuries. The general nature of their congregationalism prevented it.

At the middle of this century the Commission on Ordination of the Disciples of Christ were of the opinion that "a licensed minister has full right to perform all functions that an ordained minister may perform." Its members consider ordination "unless revoked for cause" to be for life. But licensing "is for a limited period of time and its issuance is not attended by any formal service as a rule."[84] The "official" current position on licensing for the Disciples of Christ is contained in *The Imperative Is Leadership.*

> If the ministerial candidate so desires, he may receive standing as a licensed *student minister,* granting him authority for the performance of *prescribed* ministerial functions within the *region.* Requirements for licensing usually include (a) letters of support from home congregation and institutions of higher education; (b) a written personal statement indicating religious background, concepts of the church's purpose and ministry, and career objectives; (c) the act of licensing, which takes a place in a special congregational service. The candidate is licensed *indefinitely,* but his status is reviewed *annually* (emphasis mine).[85]

The emphasized words above point up the evolution of concepts of licensing in the last quarter century. A generation ago licensing was encouraged for lay preachers as well as students. With the present stress on a professional clergy in the Disciples of Christ there is little likelihood that lay preaching will be given new emphasis.

Notes to Chapter 5

1. *Christian Messenger,* Vol. I (1827), p. 79f.

2. Ronald E. Osborn, *In Christ's Place,* p. 215.

3. A. Campbell, *Christian Baptist,* Vol. I (October, 1823), p. 50.

4. *Ibid.,* (November, 1823), p. 68. See *Millennial Harbinger* (December, 1830), p. 559.

5. A. Campbell, *Christian Baptist,* Vol. I (November 3, 1823) reprint, p. 71.

6. William West, *Barton Warren Stone,* p. 133.

7. *Millennial Harbinger* (1831), p. 114.

8. A. Campbell, *Christian Baptist,* Vol. III (1825), p. 190.

9. *Ibid.,* Vol. IV, cf. p. 260.

10. W. T. Moore, *Preacher Problems* (New York: Fleming H. Revell Co., 1907), p. 7.

11. *Millennial Harbinger* (1839), p. 383.

12. C. L. Loos, "The Want of Preachers," *Millennial Harbinger* (December, 1864), p. 553.

13. T. P. Haley, "Our Ministry," *New Christian Quarterly* (October, 1893), p. 428.

14. W. T. Moore, *Preacher Problems,* pp. 9-12.

15. Robert Richardson, *Memoirs of Alexander Campbell,* Vol. I (reprint), pp. 380, 381.

16. W. R. Walker, *A Ministering Ministry* (Cincinnati: Standard Publishing, 1938), p. 156.

17. *Ibid.,* p. 176.

18. C. B. Tupper, *Called—In Honor* (St. Louis: Bethany Press, 1949), p. 46.

19. Hampton Adams, *Calling Men for the Ministry* (St. Louis: Bethany Press, 1945), cf. p. 33.

20. H. Adams, *Your Life Work—The Christian Ministry* (Indianapolis: United Christian Missionary Society, 1947), cf. pp. 6, 7.

21. D. Ray Lindley, *Apostle of Freedom,* p. 140.

22. "The Training of the Christian Ministry," Address before the 103rd Annual Convention of Christian Churches (Disciples of Christ of Georgia).

23. James D. Murch, *The Free Church,* p. 81.

24. *Education for the Christian Ministry for Tomorrow's Church* (Lexington, Ky.: Conference Report at College of the Bible, 1953), p. 64.

25. *The Scroll* (Autumn, 1953), p. 28.

26. *Lexington Theological Seminary Bulletin,* Vol. VIII, No. 7 (March, 1973), p. 2.

27. Carroll C. Cotten, *The Imperative Is Leadership,* p. 101.

28. "What Is the Ministry?" *Christian Standard* (February 4, 1973), p. 3.

29. "Recruiting for the Ministry," *The Christian* (December 27, 1964), p. 5.

30. *Ibid.*

31. P. H. Welshimer, *Welshimer's Sermons* (Cincinnati: Standard Publishing, 1927), p. 211.

32. Carroll C. Cotten, *The Imperative Is Leadership,* p 28.

33. R. W. Burns, "Winning Youth for the Ministry," *International Convention Addresses and Reports, 1952,* p. 37.

34. "Making More Preachers," *Illinois Christian News* (May 15, 1904), cf. p. 2.

35. *Millennial Harbinger* (January, 1865), p. 33.

36. *Education for the Christian Ministry for Tomorrow's Church,* p. 27.

37. *Ibid.,* cf. p. 29.

38. "Our Position on the Ministry," *Christian Standard* (September 7, 1940), n.p.

39. "That Weasel-Word, Minister," *The Christian* (September 17, 1972), n.p.

40. *Ibid.*

41. Carroll C. Cotten, *The Imperative Is Leadership,* p. 41.

42. Robert Richardson, *Memoirs of Alexander Campbell,* Vol. I (reprint), p. 391.

43. *Ibid.,* Vol. I (reprint) cf. p. 387.

44. *Discipliana,* (November, 1961), p. 59.

45. *Millennial Harbinger* (May, 1863), p. 234.

46. P. W. Swann, *The Religious Origins and Educational Qualifications of the Ministers of the Christians (New Light) and the Disciples of Christ (Reformers) from 1800-1840,* cf. p. 34.

47. *Ibid.,* p. 38.

48. *Christian Standard* (July 17, 1909), p. 1243.

49. Robert Milligan, *Scheme of Redemption* (reprint), p. 351.

50. *Ibid.,* p. 355.

51. J. E. Moseley, *Disciples of Christ in Georgia* (Christian Board of Publication, 1954, process copy of MS), pp. 139, 140.

52. W. E. Garrison, *Heritage & Destiny* (St. Louis: Bethany Press, 1961), p. 55.

53. E. West, *The Search for the Ancient Order,* Vol. II, p. 11.

54. *Gospel Advocate* (February 23, 1967), p. 118.

55. *Christian Baptist* (December 5, 1829), p. 118.

56. *Christian Baptist* (Vol. V reprint), pp. 198, 199.

57. *Ibid.*

58. W. E. Garrison and A. T. DeGroot, *The Disciples of Christ: A History,* p. 210.

59. J. Winebrenner, ed., *History of All the Religious Denominations in the United States,* p. 169.

60. R. Foster, *The Christian Register and Almanack* (1825), Portsmouth, N.H., printed by Foster.

61. *Millennial Harbinger* (February, 1845), p. 65.

62. *Millennial Harbinger* (February, 1850), p. 102.

63. W. E. Garrison and A. T. DeGroot, *The Disciples of Christ: A History,* p. 441.

64. C. C. Ware, *North Carolina Disciples of Christ* (Christian Board of Publication, 1927), p. 181.

65. *International Convention Addresses and Reports,* 1937, p. 389.

66. Clarence E. Lemmon, "An Evaluation of Our Ministry," *The Reformation of Tradition,* p. 211.

67. *Christian Standard* (July 6, 1940), p. 639.

68. "The Ordination Committee Report: A Symposium," *Christian Standard* (September 7, 1940), p. 894.

69. *Ibid.*

70. "Doctrinal Inflation," *Christian Standard* (June 5, 1943), p. 495.

71. J. D. Murch, *Christian Minister's Manual,* p. 151.

72. *Ibid.*

73. *Ibid.,* p. 161.

74. A. Campbell, *The Christian System* (reprint), p. 64.

75. J. W. McGarvey, *A Treatise on the Eldership,* p. 73.

76. *The Christian* (October 10, 1971), p. 5.

77. William J. Moore, *The New Testament Concept of the Ministry* (St. Louis: Bethany Press, 1956), p. 43.

78. *Lexington Theological Seminary Bulletin* (February, 1970).

79. *A Response to Lund* (Association for the Promotion of Christian Unity, 1952), p. 16.

80. *Fellowship,* Vol. I, No. 1 (June, 1973), p. 4.

81. William Mander, "The Ministry," *Toward Christian Union,* James Gray, ed. (Leicester, Union Committee of Churches of Christ, 1960), p. 40.

82. "Selections from the Statement on the Report of the World Conference on Faith and Order, Edinburgh 1937," *Ibid.,* p. 84.

83. C. C. Ware, *Barton Warren Stone* (St. Louis: Bethany Press, 1932), p. 180ff.

84. *Ordination–Suggested Standards and Procedures* (Indianapolis: Division of Home Missions, United Christian Missionary Society, n.d., pamphlet), p. 28.

85. Carroll C. Cotten, *The Imperative is Leadership,* p. 85.

education

Early Views and Action

Alexander Campbell's early education came from the tutoring of his scholarly father. Thomas soon saw the boy was distinguishing himself by an aloofness to the finer academic virtues and an attraction to sports and exercise. It was not until Alexander was eighteen that he experienced an extended flirtation with theology and philosophy. Gradually he began assisting his father in the Academy at Rich Hill, some ten miles from the "flourishing town of Newry." This picturesque community afforded a "distinct view of the waters of Lough Neagh."[1]

Alexander in his late teens began memorizing select passages from the Bible and well-known authors. John Locke was a favorite, especially "Letters on Toleration" and "Essay Concerning Human Understanding." He developed a great interest in ecclesiastical history. The Independents had a congregation at Rich Hill, and Alexander heard such creative thinkers as Rowland Hill, James Haldane, and John Walker.[2] These men stressed private interpretation of Scripture, repudiation of authority of creeds and synods, and the congregational form of government. Campbell studied the writings of John Glas, Robert Sandeman, Archibald McLean, Andrew Fuller, Martin Luther, John Calvin, John Wesley, Greville Ewing and others.

Thomas left for America on April 8, 1807, seeking new health. Alexander—at age nineteen—was left in charge of the academy and the family. A letter from Thomas urged the family to journey to his new home in Washington County, Western Pennsylvania. The Ship *Hibernia* set sail October 1, 1808, but was wrecked. The season being advanced, the trip was postponed until winter could pass. The family resided in Glasgow, and Alexander attended the university. Concerning sermon making, he wrote in his diary that a preacher "must be well instructed in morality and religion, and in the original tongues in which the Scriptures are written, for without them he can hardly be qualified to explain Scripture or to teach religion and morality."[3] Alexander heard Greville Ewing often in Glasgow. He studied at the university until May, 1809; and after preparations, the family sailed for America in early August. Anchor was cast in New York harbor a month later, and Thomas met his family in Philadelphia on October 7, 1809, with the proofsheets of the *Declaration and Address* in his saddlebags.

The qualifications for a preacher that Alexander penned in 1808 were continued in his more mature years. He wrote in the last volume of the *Christian Baptist:*

> I never did distain, nor did I ever cast a distainful look upon a brother because he was illiterate. Nay, so far from it, I have generally encouraged them "to improve their gifts." But I cannot compliment any illiterate man for assuming the office of an interpreter or expositor of Scripture. . . . To hear such a man expounding texts or explaining scripture, is a burlesque on the pulpit and a satire upon the age.[4]

But to be learned in Hebrew, Greek, and ecclesiastical history is not the same as to be trained as a divine! "To *make a sermon* and to *proclaim the gospel* are two things which are as different as logic and gospel."[5] Thus, "To make a sermon is as much the work of art as to make a speech at the bar, or in the forum. No man can make a good one without much study, training, and general reading. Hence Colleges and Theological Schools are necessary, absolutely necessary, to make sermonizers."[6] Teaching theology as such, said this theologian, was no part of Christian higher education for the ministry. Campbell would have nothing to do with "the abstract and metaphysical dogmas" of the theologians. He said that theological speculation of his day about the nature of Jesus came from the "dissecting knife of theological anatomists. It is the northern extreme of frigid Calvinism."[7] The Campbells, Scott, Burnet, John T. Johnson, and others had a passion for education. They brought their education with them to the frontier. But they knew that if they did not provide sources of education, the second generation Disciples would "grow up in ignorance."

Benjamin Franklin did not share Campbell's vision of an educated ministry. He did not feel ashamed of his lack of education, neither did he stand in awe of the man of culture and knowledge. He said, "Nine-tenths of all the churches built up, owes their existence to uneducated preachers—that is in the popular sense. . . . We are in favor of educating men as fast as possible, but we have no sympathy for discouraging the humble efforts of good men, though illiterate or uneducated."[8] On another occasion Franklin declared, "We have found that simply learning does not make a preacher—that many men of profound learning are not preachers and can not be preachers to profit, and men who are preachers, good and useful preachers, can not be learned men."[9]

Education also was carried on informally. Preaching, one to two hour dissertations, was an avenue of learning. J. J. Haley expressed it: "The big preachers of that day moulded the bullets for the little ones to fire." Thus budding theologians sat at the feet of the masters. "It was marvelous what a vast quantity of predigested theological material they could take in. . . . This was their Bible college, their theological seminary, and it wasn't a bad one either."[10]

A discussion of preaching will occur in a later chapter. However, it is appropriate here to point out the educational value in the frontier preaching. Campbell abandoned the denominational "textuary and formal" mode and patterned his messages after the sermons by Jesus, Paul, and Peter. He reasoned that if you want to produce the "same coin" you have to use the "same mint." Alger Morton Fitch, Jr., noted of Campbell:

> The revivalists were preaching their opinions and their experiences. The traditionalists were proclaiming their creeds and their theologies. He asked if preaching Christianity was the same as preaching Christ? If proclaiming the Holy Spirit in every paragraph was what the New Testament meant by preaching Jesus? . . . If a preacher's constant assertion that he was a gospel preacher made him one?[11]

There was meat in the messages of the Disciples preachers and it nourished and produced growth.

The debate was another popular source of information for aspiring preachers and church officers. If not as inspiring as the pulpit, it offered another expression of Brotherhood aims and aspirations. A. T. DeGroot called it the "serious American indoor sport." Alexander Campbell was the publicized master of this art. His outstanding debates were with John Walker, 1820; McCalla, 1823; Owen, 1829; Bishop Purcell, 1836; and Reverend Rice, 1843. For this latter one Henry Clay presided. Benjamin Franklin participated in more than thirty such endeavors. John S. Sweeney and O. A. Burgess were experts in this area in the last decade of the nineteenth century. Printed debates were as lengthy as 600 pages—and more.

> T. W. Caskey (1816-96) held fifty-six public debates. D. R. Dungan (1837-1920) held thirty-seven debates most of them in Nebraska and termed them a "military necessity." Henry R. Pritchard (1819-1900), Indiana stalwart engaged in forty such duels.[12]

F. D. Kershner said of Isaac Errett:

> He believed in an educated ministry and was convinced that the only escape from legalism and from hopeless reaction was to be found in more comprehensive training and study on the part of church leaders.[13]

This was not to "substitute a cold intellectualism" for the warm, sincere preacher; it was to wed consecration and scholarship. Thomas Munnell also prized learning and championed a broad, general education. He argued that an educated man finding a preacher without knowledge of basic science "would be liable to conclude that a man of so little reading might be uncultured and narrow as to religion and might refuse to hear him preach."[14]

Colleges of the Nineteenth Century

Campbell knew that God did not qualify preachers by a miracle. The sage of Bethany believed in liberal and progressive education. He considered it "superlatively uncomely" for preachers to slaughter "the King's English."[15] It was among "uneducated ministers of religion" that he witnessed most "disgusting vanity," "boyish conceit," and "inflated ambition."

> To hear an uneducated preacher or teacher of religion . . . assail the doctrine of a Luther, a Calvin, or a Wesley, and to feast himself and his audience with an exposure of the sophistry of men, eminent for learning and piety, is an ebullition of human weakness and folly more disgusting than any other which I can imagine.[16]

In 1818 Campbell set about to remedy this "ebullition of human weakness" by opening on his farm the Buffalo Seminary. It functioned only four years. There was one successful and many unsuccessful attempts by others to open colleges around 1830.[17] J. T. Jones and George Gates made a plea in the May, 1836, *Harbinger* for a meeting in Louisville to discuss the problems of setting up a brotherhood college. Campbell approved the idea, but added that he had no use of those schools of theology which have "filled the world with idle speculation, doctrinal errors, and corruptions of all sorts, terminating in discords and heresies innumerable."[18]

Barton Stone was not as critical of uneducated preachers as was Alexander Campbell. His difficulty in receiving an education may have tempered much possible criticism. He expressed, "I love learning; but it can not supply the lack of the Spirit." He believed that "both united form a complete evangelist." He said that the brotherhood "has been too much distracted from the Gospel of salvation by a thirst and exertion to imitate and equal the sects in having colleges and seminaries among us as our own."[19] But to the question if he were opposed to college education for preachers, Stone replied, "No, far from it." He saw a real need for information and education, but did "not wish to see them made a part of heaven's religion to man."[20] Stone sought to avoid in the Christian movement what he had left in the Presbyterian—a "superior order of men," the clergy over the laity.

By 1847 the Christian Connexion, which acknowledged Stone as a founder, could claim "three institutions of learning; one located at Durham, N. H., one at Starkey, N. Y., and one near Raleigh, N.C." They were also connected with the free Theological School at Meadville, Pennsylvania, where David Millard was a professor.[21]

In 1840 Bethany College was chartered as Campbell's mature expression of his philosophy of education. He stated:

Bethany College is the only College known to us in the civilized world, founded upon the Bible: It is not a theological school, founded upon human theology, nor a school of divinity, founded upon the Bible, but a literary and scientific institution, founded upon the Bible as the basis of all true science and true learning.[22]

School opened in 1841. Campbell served as president and

professor of moral science, until a few years before his death. He also taught intellectual philosophy, evidences of Christianity, and political economy.[23] Bethany was patterned somewhat after the University of Virginia, for Campbell was an admirer of Thomas Jefferson. It offered several courses of study.

The school of sacred history and moral philosophy required four years for its completion and included such studies as the evidences of Christianity, sacred history, biblical literature, ecclesiastical history, and moral philosophy. Over this school the president himself presided.[24]

There was a two year course in chemistry and belles lettres. The school of political philosophy could also be completed in two years. Mathematics and astronomy required three years. Professors at Bethany in its early days were Campbell, W. K. Pendleton, A. F. Ross, Charles Stewart, and Robert Richardson. Pendleton came from the University of Virginia.

Campbell saw a vast difference between feeding a future preacher of the gospel on a system of "modernized theology" and a balanced diet of "Bible study and Bible training." The charter of Bethany prohibited a professorship in theology. Campbell intended for the Scriptures to "be read and studied historically," accenting the moral and spiritual power in its "facets, precepts and promises."[25] He favored no specialization by the ministerial student at this time. A fear of creating a clerical class was prominent. There was, however, this concession: "A number of students have been boarded as well as educated gratuitously at Bethany College on the pledge that they devote their lives to the Christian ministry."[26]

In 1845 Campbell listed in the *Harbinger* three Disciples colleges: Bacon, Bethany, and Franklin. Bacon began at Georgetown, Kentucky, in 1836. Walter Scott, the first president, served less than a year. D. S. Burnet served as president from 1836 to 1840. Burnet then went to Hygeia Female Atheneum, seven miles from Cincinnati. Franklin College was the effort of Tolbert Fanning, a leader of the anti-society and anti-musical instrument churches. In 1849 Kentucky Female Orphan School was opened at Midway, and Western Reserve Eclectic Institute (now Hiram College) was organized at Hiram, Ohio. James A. Garfield was its second president. Fairview Academy, opened in 1843, was the forerunner of Butler University, and 1855 saw the opening of Christian University, now Culver-Stockton College. Hesperian College, 1860, became Chapman College at Los Angeles. Dozens of colleges came into being. Some died in infancy, others before adolescence, a few more in their awkward teens. A small percentage reached maturity. A. T. DeGroot wrote:

> Soon the prairies were scattered with the bones of dead colleges whose very names have been forgotten. It is not surprising that the Disciples of that period little realized what it took to make a college, in money, scholarship, and constituency. Academic standards were low, secondary schools were almost non-existent, and teachers were cheap. But education was a magic word and great sacrifices were made that the church might have its colleges, of what ever grade.[27]

The extent of college training among the better known preachers in the second half of the nineteenth century and beginning of the twentieth century is indicated by the men whom W. T. Moore chose for his preaching volumes of 1868 and 1918. Sermons from twenty-nine men were in the *Living Pulpit of the Christian Church.* Of these, twelve were graduates of Bethany college, but ten of the twenty-nine, one-third, had no college training.[28] By comparison, *The New Living Pulpit* featured twenty-eight prominent preachers in 1918, and only two were without college training. "Eight had college training but no degrees, eight had stopped with A.B. Degrees, five had masters degrees, two had Bachelor of Divinity degrees, and two had Ph.D. Degrees."[29]

The Practical Situation

The rank and file on the frontier were not as captivated by the spirit of Minerva as were the Campbells. F. M. Lowe, Jr., phrased it more frankly. "The preachers were not only itinerant, but, at least from the point of view of higher education, illiterate proclaimers of the Word."[30] This description makes its point, with some hyperbole. Many lacked formal education, but they respected the Biblical languages. W. E. Garrison has surmised that more preachers read their Greek New Testament in 1860 than in 1960.

Preaching was the foundation for the Christians, upholding a structure of revivalism and "personal entreaty." With the development of the evangelistic procedures of Walter Scott, preaching became major among the Reformers also. As the movement grew rapidly, often large portions of a congregation at a time transferred membership, new converts ringing old ideas into the brotherhood. The educational aims of some of the founding fathers were then turned aside by the press of circumstances.

P. W. Swann made a study for his B.D. thesis on educational qualifications of sixty pioneer preachers. Twenty-eight of the sixty were designated as "self-educated," having no specific academic training; fourteen had taken academic training; fifteen received university education; eight had a theological background; and nine were professionally educated.[31] A few men enjoyed the privilege of more than one avenue of education. If such a ratio can be applied to all of the pioneer preachers, then nearly fifty percent were uneducated or self-educated.

In spite of the zeal for founding colleges, seminaries, and female schools, the ministerial educational level was low. Founding a college and presenting an adequate curriculum are not the same. Founding a college and maintaining one properly are far from identical. Garrison and DeGroot contend that a major difficulty was that "the colleges themselves were isolated from the main intellectual currents of the time."[32] As far as Bethany College was concerned, Campbell considered agrarian seclusion to be an asset rather than a liability. Many of the pioneer leaders were impressed with the Corinthian observation, "how that not many wise men after the flesh, not many mighty, not many noble are called." Clinton Lockhart, a noted educator and college president, felt otherwise:

> Had our earlier colleges been stronger, the demand for more extensive instruction would have been so great that we would have been forced to supply it. . . . The reason the demand is not greater is, that we have few preachers among us who have taken such a course so as to lead others to seek it.[33]

Sowers went forth to sow "college seed," but too much fell along the path, the rocky ground, and in the thorns.

Lack of formal education may not have been too great a handicap for evangelism along the frontier to one with great natural ability and possessing a vision, such as Raccoon John Smith or Jacob Creath. Of Creath it was said, "Like Smith, he was a man of but little culture, but of great natural power. He was, perhaps, the most eloquent preacher of his day, and one of the most tender-hearted and affectionate of men."[34] But initial evangelism is a partial gospel, the frontier passes, and religious geniuses are scarce. As early as 1840 vigorous voices were pleading the cause of better ministerial education.[35]

The Changing Scene

Campbell's aversion to theological study *per se* for ministerial training was generally accepted in the Brotherhood for many years. He knew well these systems of thought, but many of his imitators know only his denunciation. How widely and in what depth Campbell read can be gleaned from the "Short Title List" of the books in his library, as prepared by Charles Penrose. Thus when education was accented in the 1830's to 1850's it was seldom done with speculative theology in mind. Forceful Ben Franklin illustrated this as he described a man's educational qualifications for the ministry. "He must have a Bible education. He must especially have a New Testament education. He must have a gospel education."[36]

In 1856 Isaac Errett voiced reasoned criticism of the Bethany plan of preparation of preachers.

> There should be a school of prophets—a theological school—where men of learning and wisdom, and large experience could impart the sum of their knowledge, from books, from life, and from their own souls, to the young and prepare them for wise and fruitful labors.[37]

In the late 1850's and 1860's many debates arose among segments of the brotherhood concerning the direction of the "ancient order of things" and "the propriety of special education for preachers." Out of this type of criticism and analysis came the idea for the college of the Bible. It began because certain brotherhood leaders saw the needs of a seminary course of instruction. F. D. Kershner explained, "He (Campbell) could have had no more loyal adherents than

Loos, Milligan and McGarvey, but these men saw clearly that the Campbell program for ministerial education was hopelessly inadequate."[38] J. W. McGarvey studied at Bethany from 1847-1850. But when he left, as he stated on several occasions, he felt "unprepared for the work. I had insufficient general knowledge, and insufficient experience in public speaking." In 1865 he penned:

> The young preacher should have a course of instruction, in special preparation for his work, which would not be appropriate for other young men. This can be accomplished by a separate school or by a separate department of the same school.[39]

J. J. Haley says in his history of the movement, "A Bible College where the Bible is the textbook, to be directly studied and taught, was the conception of Prof. McGarvey and its establishment the greatest achievement of his life. This institution was for a long time the only real Bible College in the world."[40]

Benjamin Franklin opposed the start of a theological school and carried his position in the *American Christian Review.* He believed that an apprentice system should prevail, much as young men studied law and medicine. Franklin, Tolbert Fanning, and David Lipscomb all were of the belief that there was little or no good in "theological seminaries." Schools set aside solely to prepare preachers were infringing upon the domain of the church.

The center of leadership in the cooperative brotherhood was already passing from Bethany to Lexington, Kentucky, when Kentucky University moved to Lexington in 1865. The College of the Bible, presided over by Robert Milligan, was one of five colleges of the university. J. W. McGarvey was a professor of Bible; John B. Bowman was regent of the university. The open conflict between Bowman and the Board of Curators on one side, and J. W. McGarvey and Moses E. Lard on the other, with a vigorous assist from Ben Franklin and David Lipscomb, will not be analyzed here. It concerned politics, university management, and personality conflicts, as much as educational philosophy. The result was that an independent college of the Bible was formed in 1877, and in 1878 the university finally permitted it to use its classrooms.

The controversy, raging in the 1870's, convinced Franklin

and Lipscomb that colleges could "be a source of evil as well as good." Lipscomb sided with Fanning in his educational debates with Alexander Campbell. Lipscomb wrote in 1875:

> We think the most fatal mistake of Alexander Campbell's life, and one that has done much and we fear will do much more to undo his life's work, was the establishment of a school to train and educate young preachers. . . . We think the idea of taking young men and withdrawing them in a preacher's school to make preachers of them, results in evil in many ways, without one particle of good attached. Christ did not take his teachers from that class.[41]

This viewpoint saw higher education resulting in "pedantic striplings who prate about the illiteracy of our ablest men." The leaders viewed the Bible college approach in the same vein as did Campbell the theological seminaries forty years previously. A related theory was that endowments of colleges were evil as they permitted the schools to rely on money, rather than the Bible and the brotherhood. Projecting this disturbance over higher education, Earl West observed in 1950: "The Churches of Christ have not yet outgrown the full effect of the troubles at Kentucky University nor are they likely to do so in this generation."[42]

Daniel Sommer (1850-1940) was a successor to Ben Franklin. He is considered one of the patriarchs of the churches of Christ. He studied at Bethany under Pendleton, Loos, and Richardson, but their views only hardened his concepts of apostolic discipline and absolutism. Sommer left Bethany in 1872 without taking final exams. He soon earned the reputation of "critic of brotherhood activities," but Franklin saw him as "one of the most promising young men in my whole acquaintance."[43] Sommer had great influence on the educational criteria for the anti-organ brethren. Earl West concludes:

> Sommer's experiences at Bethany College found him departing from school with absolute disgust at the idea that a preacher needed a college education. . . . Sommer could never think of himself in any role except the successor of Elder Ben Franklin, whom he regarded as the greatest gospel preacher since apostolic times. Franklin in his later years opposed colleges, and the man who wore his mantle would be likely to do the same.[44]

David Lipscomb gave deeper insight into church of Christ educational philosophy when he noted in 1877:

> We have always believed in Bible schools, Bible academies, and Bible colleges. . . . Our objection to Bible college has been that they were especially to make preachers. The evil of the churches, the corrupting influence is found, we are sure, in the position of the preachers and the tendency to subject everything in the churches to the work of the preacher.[45]

David Lipscomb and James A. Harding, after several years of dreaming and praying, opened the Nashville Bible School in 1891. Thirty-two students were enrolled the first session. Two months before it opened, Lipscomb aired a proposal "to open a school in Nashville." "Safe and competent teachers" were to fulfill the aim "to teach the Christian religion as presented in the Bible in its purity and fullness; and in teaching this to prepare Christians for usefulness, in whatever sphere they are called upon to labor."[46] The accent was: no exclusive preparation for preachers. Professionalism was to be kept a devil's distance from the preachers. Every student was required to attend at least one Bible class daily. Lipscomb taught New Testament; Harding led the other departments. In its early years the school awarded no degrees, only a "diploma book," for Harding had a strong aversion to "empty titles." When Harding moved to Bowling Green, Kentucky, Lipscomb incorporated the school and began to confer the "literary and scientific degrees common in the college and higher institutions of learning."[47]

Daniel Sommer, editor of *Octographic Review,* saw this later move as one of mischief. He felt that colleges by nature encouraged an advancement of the status of preachers and thus mischief for the church. His idea of education was the original Buffalo Seminary that Campbell conducted from his home. However, fire flashed and within a few years a dozen similar Bible colleges sprang up among the brethren.

Sommer and Lipscomb have raised progeny to this day, and the controversy has not ceased among the leaders in the churches of Christ over the relationship of the church to education. Earl West admits that "personalities, sectional pride and prejudice have played no small part in keeping the question alive."[48]

Evolution in College Curriculums

While the group later to be gathered under the churches of Christ segment were forming their philosophy of ministerial education, other voices, as Clinton Lockhart, received a wider hearing in the brotherhood. He believed that graduate studies in "Theology, Biblical Criticism, Sacred Literature" and "Semitic Languages" were "almost indispensable to him who would accomplish the best results."[49] Good ministerial education was to Lockhart the key to the church's prosperity. Ignorance here was worse than weakness; it was disgrace.

At the turn of the century few leaders demanded educational standards for entrance into the professional ministry. Many persons maintained a suspicious attitude toward any suggestion of definite academic training. But there slowly rose the rolling tide of greater education—graduate education—for the Disciples of Christ. Lockhart and Ames received the first doctorate degrees in 1894 and 1895 from Yale University and University of Chicago respectively. Since then the doctorate has been the goal of most Disciples educators. Yet these degrees, until quite recently, have not been in the field of theology. The interests were Biblical, philosphical, and practical.

In spite of this awareness of educational needs in the cooperative groups, a survey reveals that by 1930 only 11.1 percent of the ministers had received post-graduate training; and 56.6 percent held college degrees.[50] However, this does not reflect a treadmill result during one hundred years. Half of the preachers being uneducated or self-educated in 1840 is quite different from half not finishing college in 1930. Academically, in 1840 the movement was sprouting seeds nursery style; in 1930 it was cultivating a new forest in deeper soil. In 1935 E. S. Ames pointed out the direction to be taken by the Disciples of Christ:

> The only way to be guarded against the errors of theological and philosphical thought is to be familiar with the theology and philosophy. The Disciples have tried to escape theology by being ignorant of it.[51]

The thought advanced was that the minister must be an educator and counselor as well as preacher. The emphasis was that the training received determines to a large degree just how God will use a man. F. D. Kershner of Butler University held the thesis that the colleges had operated under three successive philosphies: the undifferentiated, the differentiated, and the standardized. He saw them as three distinct phases.[52] His categories will be utilized in this evolution of college curriculums.

The undifferentiated period started with Bacon College in 1836, and Bethany was firmly committed to it. Campbell's dislike of dogma became his distrust of theology as taught in the eastern universities. His idea of ministerial education was a good four-year course accenting the study of Scripture and related religious subjects. F. D. Kershner reminds us that a good college degree on the frontier one hundred and forty years ago "meant considerable education."[53] Benjamin Franklin wrote: "The college educates no matter whether for preachers, for lawyers, doctors, merchants, or farmers."[54] Campbell saw Bible study in a broad spectrum of learning:

> Lectures on the Bible are lectures on the antiquities of the world; on creation itself; on language; on man as he was, on man as he is, on man as he will hereafter be; on the foundation of states, and the fortune of empires. They are lectures upon sacred geography, chronology, and the ancient policies, manners, customs and usages.[55]

Creeds and speculative theology to Bethany's father were deemed worse than useless. The New Testament contained the gospel; it was the Word. Under this philosophy it was not unique to find preachers who could quote the New Testament from memory.

Colleges following the undifferentiated concept included Hiram College, founded in 1850; North Western Christian University (later Butler University), founded in 1855; Eureka College, begun in 1855: and Add-Ran Christian College (parent of Texas Christian University).

The differentiated period came into being with the opening of the College of the Bible at Lexington, Kentucky, in 1865. This college was really a "seminary which did not confine its attention to the Bible exclusively, but which did emphasize the Sacred text and was decidedly short in the study of theology proper."[56] Former teachers of the Bethany plan were leaders in this new interpretation: Robert Richardson, first president of College of the Bible, and W. K. Pendleton, second president of Bethany. In 1855 Bethany appointed J. P. Robinson and Isaac Errett to solicit funds for a new building and professorship for a "more thorough and systematic course of instruction for the education of men to preach the gospel."[57] W. K. Pendleton believed that opposition to this approach of specialized study was fostered by a "reformation-prejudice" against theological schools. This approach was not designed to advance speculative theology, but to further "ministerial education." His argument to Ben Franklin was:

> The ordinary college course is a process of general education: the after work of training a young man for the ministry is only a continuation of his education in a further and special direction. The difference is not between *educating* a young man and *making* a preacher of him—but between a *general* and a *special* one.[58]

The differentiated theory was not without opposition from those other than the fundamentalistic brethren. In 1846 articles appeared in the *Harbinger* advocating "preacher schools" for training of men wanting to evangelize, but not wanting the discipline or time-cost of a strict college education. Campbell allowed different religious views a voice in his journal. However, he replied to these advocates and said such schools were "lean and decrepit substitutes for colleges and universities worthy of the name."[59] The *New Christianity Quarterly* featured an article in 1893 in which the cry against the "meager facilities for the education of our ministry" was met with the retort to use fully the available resources before charging "the inefficiency and ignorance of the ministry on the absence of schools for higher education among the Disciples."[60]

The educational sweep was with this differentiated Bowman-Milligan plan, and Drake University (1881) adopted it when it began in Des Moines, Iowa. E. V. Zollars and Frank Marshall favored this philosophy when founding the College of the Bible at Oklahoma Christian University (now Phillips University) in 1906. Brite College of the Bible followed it at Texas Christian University. In 1924 Butler University gave up its department of religion in the College of Arts and Science to form the School of Religion.[61] Other educational units followed this approach. In Britain the ministry heightened professional training in the founding of Overdale College, Selly Oak, Birmingham, England, in 1920. A good survey of Disciples of Christ growth in these ideals is seen in Garrison and DeGroot, *The Disciples of Christ: A History.*

The third period was the standardized. Its beginning came with the organization of the American Association of Theological Schools around 1930. We recall that all Disciples colleges were founded independently of each other, either by private or community initiative, or by regional church segment. In 1914 twenty-six institutions did affiliate with the newly formed Board of Education of Disciples of Christ. By 1939 the Board of Higher Education was chartered to enlarge the prior work. By 1950 thirty-seven colleges, seminaries, and Bible chairs were members of this board on a voluntary basis. In 1973 there were twenty-three related institutions having membership in the board. Fourteen are colleges, four are universities, and five are related Bible chairs and schools of religion.

The Disciples of Christ institutions seek accreditation in top regional and national associations, as part of their philosophy of education. This segment does not view this conformity to certain curriculum ideals as a limitation of quality desired. The structured Disciples see standardization as accenting their education aims. The tendency in the past decade for Disciples of Christ and other denominations has been to view the seminary as dedicated to the program of professional ministerial education, not graduate study of religion, philosophy, and theology. The 1966 study by Charles R. Fielding, *Education for Ministry,* has given direction to this approach. The accent here is to relate the graduate seminarian with "groups to whom they must relate as clergymen"— community leaders, social conflict groups, denominational agencies and boards, and ecumenical endeavors. This trend in course study is carried forward to new expressions in the offering of degrees. The traditional Bachelor of Divinity (B.D.) degree representing three years of graduate study has been replaced in Disciples seminaries with the Master of Divinity degree (M.Div.). This is considered the "first professional degree." However, there is no present agreement as to the requirements for the Doctor of Ministry (D.Min.). Some institutions award it as the second professional degree, requiring a minimum of one year beyond the M.Div. Two of the foundation houses give the D.Min. as a four-year degree, in lieu of the three-year M.Div. The great majority of Disciples of Christ graduates take a preaching or administrative post following the receipt of the first professional degree, although an increasing number continue on to receive the D.Min.

Many Disciples of Christ students enroll in seminaries throughout North America. Most of these are at Yale Divinity School, Union Theological Seminary, New York, and Pacific School of Religion in Berkeley, California. A concomitant result is seen in the non-Disciples of Christ enrolled in Disciples institutions.

> In 1961, 76 percent of the students enrolled in Disciples seminaries were Disciples (range 61 percent to 93 percent among the seminaries). In 1972, 51 percent of the students were Disciples (range 34 percent to 75 percent).[62]

While the Disciples of Christ seminaries continue to train the majority of the professional ministers of this group, they are providing training to an increasing number of ministers of other denominations.

Four accredited seminaries are related to the Disciples of Christ. In the 1971-1972 year fifty-seven full-time and thirteen part-time professors were on the faculties. Of these seventy men, forty-four or 63 percent have an earned doctor's degree. This educational emphasis for the faculty is not found to the same degree among the Christian churches and the churches of Christ. It is also interesting that three of the fourteen related colleges produced more than 50 percent of the Disciples students enrolled in the seminaries in the decade of 1961 to 1971: Northwest Christian College, Phillips University, and Texas Christian University.[63]

The Independent Colleges

The 1906 split between the Disciples and the churches of Christ had been on the horizon for at least three decades. Factors contributing to this division included the loss of Alexander Campbell's leadership and influence, geographical and economic separation, the organ issue, open communion controversy, the missionary organization question, reactionary editorial policies, the settled pastor controversy, and emphasis on the education of the ministry. J. W. Shepherd and David Lipscomb made the formal break with the *Preacher's List* of "loyal" preachers. The listings made in 1906 and 1907 indicate that the churches of Christ view represented 13 percent of the membership, 24 percent of the churches, and 24 percent of the preachers. However, in Tennessee, Texas, Arkansas, and Alabama, the anti-brethren were in the majority. The growth of the churches of Christ was rapid for certain periods. The "loyal ministers list" grew from 657 in 1906 to 1,400 in 1909, to 2,300 in 1915. However, by 1930 the list had only advanced to 2,400. Dissension was within their ranks, concerning the objection to Sunday schools, use of literature for Bible study, authority of the preacher, missions, order of worship, and use of Communion cups.

There remained within the fold of the Disciples, during the churches of Christ departure, a sizeable number of congregations and ministers who were deeply concerned with "innovations" by the progressive elements of the brotherhood. However, they refused to make an issue or test of fellowship over the settled pastor concept or the use of instrumental music. They were largely fundamental in their theology, and looked askance at technical ministerial education. W. E. Garrison described this climate: "Not all churches want educated ministers. Not all young men entering the ministry want more than the indispensable minimum of education."[64]

The first educator to put this independent philosophy into effect was Ashley S. Johnson who founded Johnson Bible College at Kimberlin Heights, Tennessee, in 1893. He explained:

> We hear much in our time about a "trained ministry," a "theological education," "an educated pulpit." It is a fact beyond discussion that much of the training of preachers is in the wrong direction—away from the masses. Jesus called His Apostles, ordained them, and immediately sent them into the field—back to the people.[65]

The next such school was Minnesota Bible College, 1913, followed in 1919 by the Kentucky Christian College. Five more began in the 1920's, and two more in the following decade. The issue that began the second visible division in the brotherhood was the open membership controversy. In 1919 in a proposal for a united church of Christ in China, Frank Garrett, secretary of the China Mission, wrote to the Executive Committee of the Foreign Christian Missionary Society and suggested the reasonableness of open membership, accepting members without immersion. C. S. Medbury, chairman of the committee, responded, vetoing the idea. In the issue of August 7, 1920, the *Christian Standard* published an article by R. E. Elmore charging China missionaries with open membership. Then during the 1922 International Convention, John T. Brown charged that his recent China visit revealed the practice of open membership. The matter went unsettled for several years. The 1926 convention, after receiving a three-man report of their trip abroad, declared open membership discontinued and censured Brown for a "careless manner" in his prior report.

As a result of what the *Christian Standard* called a dearth of "fair play or common sense action," a Committee on Future Action was appointed, including W. R. Walker, P. H. Welshimer, and W. E. Sweeney. Their decision was to commence a new national convention to foster fellowship and proclaim the gospel without conducting agency business. During the first North American Christian Convention in Indianapolis in October, 1927, W. E. Sweeney stated:

> The primary object of this convention is that members of the entire brotherhood be given an opportunity of assembling here to take part in and hear a restatement of the fundamental principles for which, we, as a people, stand.

In the 1929 North American Christian Convention, P. H. Welshimer as chairman, stated: "This convention is not in opposition to the International Convention recently held in Seattle. It is not a gathering of a bunch of folk who have split off from anything."[66] In spite of Welshimer's idealism, the *Restoration Herald* and the *Christian Standard* in the following years began to proclaim the differences between the International Convention and the North American Christian Convention as more than a problem of business and promotion—an issue "directly related to the entire problem of fellowship."[67]

The Commission on Restudy of the Disciples of Christ made an effort in 1941, without success, to unite the two conventions. Some national leaders made appearances at both for years. However, the brotherhood was polarizing to the extent that the *Christian Standard* could declare in 1942, "The North American Convention's only reason for existence is the failure of the International Convention to be the sort of meeting that gives our movement a message and an inspiration."[68] The *Standard* championed the North American and the *Christian-Evangelist* supported the International, with ministers generally taking sides. The 1942 North American displayed a spirit of suspicion and unrest. The *Standard* observed, "There was strong opposition to the presence on the program of any person in any way supporting the United Society or any board affiliated with the International Convention."[69]

This hasty overview of the North American Convention serves as background to the growing tension between conservative and progressive leadership among the Disciples. The North American did not meet during the war years of 1943-1945, yet in this period there was an outcropping of nine more "preacher-training" schools. It is a fair evaluation to say that the Bible schools founded after 1942 were a protest against the International Convention, the United Christian Missionary Society, and the Board of Higher Education.[70]

The Bible college movement seemed to the advocates of the Board of Higher Education to be an effort to "determine the character of the ministry among the Disciples."[71] Conservative congregations became aware that several of the cooperative schools were not educating their share of the ministers needed. For example, Lincoln Bible Institute filled a vacuum that Eureka College had produced through seeming lack of concern. Many congregations insisted on Bible-quoting, Bible-preaching pastors, and if the cooperative college programs appeared inadequate to develop this approach, the churches would have them anyway.

In the 1940's and 1950's the educational attributes of the faculties of most of the Bible colleges produced an unbalanced curriculum. Professorships were in the field of religion, and usually instructors taught full-time in the arts and sciences. Thus some educators believed an atmosphere of apologetics, in the common sense, was created for the sciences and church history. Again, because the professors were often inbred, teaching at their own schools after little or no advance education, there was scant encouragement for their students to seek graduate study elsewhere. A 1953 survey of 4,457 ministers showed 1,645 graduates of accredited seminaries, but only 112 of these were of the Christian church allegiance.[72] This ratio study led many to fear that the "Independent" (Christian church) educational philosophy had slipped into indoctrination, with its corresponding fear of a critical education in religion. When one preaches dogma without discernment, it becomes schismatic. An occasional voice spoke for depth and discernment in this period. Eugene P. Price penned for the *Christian Standard* in 1954:

> The minister should be the product of a liberal education. To be trained for the ministry and to be educated for the ministry are by no means synonymous expressions. A minister may receive adequate Bible training and still be uneducated for the ministry.[73]

The publication of the 1955 *A Directory of the Ministry of the Undenominational Fellowship of Christian Churches and Churches of Christ* by Vernon M. Newland, formally declared another split in the historic Campbell-Stone Movement. The "Foreword" stated, "Not the publication of this Directory, but the need for it, is the greater tragedy." The tragedy was, to Newland, the desertion of the Campbellian concepts by the Disciples of Christ. This yearly directory has served since its inception as the identification of the ministry of the Christian churches, and promotes the Bible college institutions. The *Christian Standard* has periodically identified these "loyal schools" through the years. In 1941 the *Standard* recognized only thirteen loyal Bible schools, explaining that the criteria was "those institutions that we understand to be definitely committed to the Restoration cause."[74] This list included College of the Bible, Phillips University, and College of Religion, Butler University. In 1946, eighteen colleges were designated; in 1951, twenty-two colleges were named; and in 1965, thirty-five Bible institutions were listed in the *Standard,* containing more than 2,500 students preparing for some type of religious work. A list of the current educational institutions affiliated with each of the three branches of the Campbell-Stone Movement is contained in the Appendix of *Thoughts on Unity.* The *Lookout* for November 19, 1972, gave this summary from a 1972 survey: Total enrollment of twenty-eight Bible colleges, 5,837; enrollment of three graduate seminaries, 331; student body of Milligan College, 730; for a grand total of 6,898 students. Standard Publishing supplied these figures for 1974: thirty-four Bible colleges with an enrollment of 7,034; three graduate seminaries with 537 students; and Milligan College with 748 enrolled. The grand total is 8,319.[75]

While the general trend of denominational religious institutions was a decline in enrollment, between 1972 and 1974 there were six new Bible colleges listed, with the total enrollment in the Bible colleges showing an increase of 18 percent. The three graduate seminaries increased their student bodies 62 percent during the same period. In 1971 one out of three of the 546 men and women graduating from Bible colleges went on to graduate work. Edwin V. Hayden noted that not only is there a new interest in graduate work, but there is a growing awareness of a specialized ministry among the Christian churches.

New churches are being born at a rate exceeding one hundred a year, and some of these are attracting our most capable ministers. New missionaries are going out at a similar rate. And churches once served by one preaching minister are now using two, three and even four full-time workers in various special fields.[76]

The Bible college is admittedly a "single-purpose school." The regional accrediting associations until recently would not accredit such a school. There came into being in 1947 the American Association of Bible Colleges, a nationally accepted crediting agency for church vocation schools. In 1967 there were forty-five accredited schools and fifteen associate schools of all denominations in the association out of two hundred such Bible schools in North America. As of 1972 seven Christian church colleges had been accepted into AABC. Any accrediting association by analyzing and overseeing faculty, facilities, libraries and curriculum and finances, gives status and prestige to its members. Twenty years ago seeking such accreditation would have caused concern among the "loyal brethren" for such effort.

In the 1940's and 1950's there was obvious tension between the Bible colleges and the Disciples colleges associated with the Board of Higher Education. It was a common belief of the Bible-college faculties that they were commissioned to counteract the liberal tendencies they saw developing in the Disciples institutions. Again, the Bible colleges were seeking greater enrollment, and with new colleges appearing almost yearly, there was a continuous appeal to the churches to send students.

As a result of these philosophies, two conditions prevailed in many of the Bible colleges. First, there was a cursory approach to the theologies of the neo-orthodox and existentialist thinkers such as Barth, Brunner, Kierkegaard, Tillich, Maritain, Berdyaev, and Niebuhr. There was an avoidance of the original works of most non-evangelical religious leaders. Reliance was placed largely upon older conservative Biblical works, including the nineteenth-century writings of the restoration movement.

The second condition was that faculties and college libraries often were not adequate to handle the influx of students, and the quality of education suffered. Beginning with a philosophy that ministry is primarily preaching and preaching is largely from the heart, the result was graduating men with a zeal but without adequate knowledge and experience. A good fisherman not only loves to fish, he knows the best equipment and when and where to use it.

W. E. Garrison was not too charitable in his evaluation of the educational aims of the "Independent Movement" of this period. They

> established a great many "Bible Seminaries" for the quick training of as many young men as possible to carry on a ministry based upon the traditional slogans and the unscrutinized presuppositions of early nineteenth-century religion and the principles of restoration in a rigid mold. Fundamentalism became the rule of faith of this segment.[77]

In the 1960's and 1970's several of the more established colleges began to re-examine their purpose and methods. Just "preaching the gospel" was deemed inadequate for a mature minister. Ministerial education took on a wider dimension. This does not mean that there is a strong advocacy for a liberal arts philosophy. Milligan College in Tennessee is the only four-year liberal arts college among the Christian churches. The goal, as expressed by Daniel T. Johnson, is "we must dedicate our colleges to being the best in educating a total ministry for the church." Johnson views the future of the church-related college as meeting the needs of the man in the pew with his accent on technical education.

If we are to survive in the growing failure of private colleges, we must dream. Either we must concentrate on our small but good preacher-educating colleges with a spin-off of educationists, musicians, etc., or we will expand our endeavors to encompass the pew as well as the pulpit in order to carry out world evangelism and service to the local community.[78]

Harold W. Ford, of Cincinnati Bible Seminary, struck a new note when he wrote, "Our Bible colleges should be purposefully increasing their selectivity in admitting students to programs of study . . . our concern should be for an increasing level of quality in the students. . . ."[79] He sees this as an era where the Bible college is exceeding the level of instruction in the liberal arts college, and thus the church institutions should demand "students of an extraordinary sort." This includes a "dedication to study and preparation as will make him an efficient servant of Jesus Christ."[80]

We should seek the student, from whatever background, who is dedicated to Christ and the church and whose dedication works in him a diligent pursuit in the sources of knowledge available to him in a college of such nature. We should seek the student who is not fearful to study the Bible in relationship to the learning of men and who is concerned to pursue all learning lest some unapproached area of learning be the one which, if investigated, would upset his Christian balance.[81]

Hampton Adams expressed a similar idea for the Disciples of Christ twenty-seven years prior, "The cause of much incompetence in the ministry is the great haste with which some men have entered this most demanding calling."[82] The sacredness of the ministry should prevent a mature Christian from entering into it unless willing to pay the price of adequate preparation. For the Christian churches neither the "Bethany plan" nor the "College of the Bible plan" is followed. The Bible college philosophy does not embrace the position of C. L. Loos in 1865 that called for a general college education and then ministerial specialization.[83] Most of the educators favor an upgraded four-year course, with a major in Bible, and adequate liberal arts training. The great majority of the graduates do not go directly into advanced study, and the needs of the pastorate must be met.

The Christian churches are still plagued with the consequences of too much individualism, as seen in the springing up of embryonic educational endeavors almost overnight, and their being thrust upon the church's doorstep as helpless children, with the implication of a duty of fatherhood. The Christian churches ministry comes out of its own colleges. This segment of the movement will do well to keep expanding its vision as to faculty and curriculum, regardless of the sacrifice. There is need of development in fields of church history, theology, philosophy, and the sciences. The minister of this day cannot afford the provincialism of narrow specialization.

Churches of Christ Education

The first progenitor of the educational philosophy of the churches of Christ was Franklin College, founded by Tolbert Fanning in 1845 east of Nashville, Tennessee, when he was thirty-five years old. Thomas Campbell founded Bethany college when he was fifty-two. Although Fanning was encouraged in this pursuit by Campbell and held many of Campbell's educational ideas at first, he was gradually to develop a philosophy of education that resulted in severe criticism of the "Campbell system." The oldest existing college affiliated with the churches of Christ is David Lipscomb, founded in 1891 as the Nashville Bible School by James A. Harding and David Lipscomb. After stating the purpose "to prepare Christians for usefulness" Lipscomb added:

> Such additional branches of learning will be taught as are needful and helpful in understanding and obeying the Bible and in teaching it to others.[84]

The churches of Christ colleges that followed David Lipscomb College adhered to the two basic concepts that guided the school on Granny White Pike: the Bible is part of every course of study; and the college is not exclusively a preacher preparation school. It has been generally held that theological education is no criteria for effective gospel preaching. Professional schools were believed to have the sinful tendency of "lording it over God's heritage." There has continued in many areas of this segment of the movement the sentiment of Daniel Sommer, stated in 1893:

Collegism among disciples led to preacherism, and preacherism led to organism and societyism, and these led to worldliness in the Church.[85]

Abilene Christian College began in 1906 as Childers' Classical Institute. A wave of colleges swept across the south at the turn of the century, and like earlier Disciples colleges, as many died as survived. At present there are six four-year colleges associated with the churches of Christ, and some fifteen junior colleges, of which one is in Japan and two in Canada.

This decade has seen an expansion in education philosophy in many of these institutions. The view of Sommer that a college is often the root of much evil has lost adherents. More and more scholars are seeking advanced degrees in "secular" universities. Leroy Garrett, professor at Bishop College in Dallas, has made this summary evaluation:

The Church of Christ schools are liberal arts centered, after the Campbell tradition, and more like the Disciples schools, but unlike the Independent's Bible colleges, albeit more conservative and more parochial than the Disciples. Abilene Christian College, Pepperdine, Lipscomb, Harding, and now Oklahoma Christian are all accredited and follow a traditional liberal arts curriculum. There are Bible departments and ministerial programs, but these are within the liberal arts program. The most recent trend is graduate theological training, which are clerical training institutions for the most part. There are now two of these: Harding Graduate School of Religion in Memphis, and graduate program of religion at Abilene, both of which offer the equivalent of the old B.D. degree. Several Bible Chair programs at universities are moving in new and creative directions.[86]

Notes to Chapter 6

1. Robert Richardson, *Memoirs of Alexander Campbell,* Vol. I (Standard Publishing, reprint), p. 31.

2. *Ibid.,* p. 60.

3. *Ibid.,* p. 138.

4. *Christian Baptist,* Vol. VII (July, 1830) reprint, p. 299.

5. *Ibid.,* p. 184.

6. *Ibid.,* p. 185.

7. *Ibid.,* Vol. II, p. 169.

8. Otis L. Castleberry, *They Heard Him Gladly* (Old Paths Publishing Co., 1963), p. 41.

9. *Ibid.,* p. 42.

10. J. J. Haley, *Makers and Molders of the Reformation Movement,* 1914 (College Press: Restoration Reprint Library, reprint), pp. 123, 124.

11. Alger Morton Fitch, Jr., *Alexander Campbell* (Austin: Sweet Publishing Co., 1970), p. 27.

12. W. E. Garrison and A. T. DeGroot, *The Disciples of Christ: A History,* p. 383.

13. *Christian Standard* (June 20, 1940), p. 690.

14. Thomas Munnell, *The Care of All the Churches,* p. 228.

15. *Millennial Harbinger* (March, 1835), cf. p. 135.

16. *Ibid.* (May, 1843), p. 213; also p. 214.

17. W. E. Garrison and A. T. DeGroot, *op. cit.,* cf. pp. 250-253.

18. *Millennial Harbinger* (May, 1836), p. 201. See also E. S. Ames statement in *International Convention Addresses and Reports,* 1938, p. 229.

19. J. M. Mathes, *Works of Elder B. W. Stone* (Cincinnati: Moore, Wilstoch, Keys and Co., 1859), p. 200.

20. *Ibid.,* See also J. Winebrenner, *op. cit.,* p. 169.

21. J. Winebrenner, *op. cit.,* cf. p. 169.

22. *Millennial Harbinger* (May, 1850), p. 291.

23. Robert Richardson, *Memoirs of Alexander Campbell* Vol. II (reprint), p. 485.

24. Perry E. Gresham, ed., *The Sage of Bethany* (St. Louis: Bethany Press, 1960), p. 20.

25. *Millennial Harbinger* (January, 1855), cf. p. 9.

26. *Ibid.* (September, 1857), p. 526.

27. W. E. Garrison and A. T. DeGroot, *The Disciples of Christ: A History*, p. 253.

28. C. E. Lemmon, "An Evaluation of Our Ministry," *The Reformation of Tradition*, p. 206.

29. *Ibid.*, p. 207.

30. F. M. Lowe, *The Pastorate Among the Disciples of Christ*, (St. Louis: Bethany Press, 1923), p. 38.

31. P. W. Swann, *The Religious Origins and Educational Qualifications of the Ministers of the Christian (New Lights) and the Disciples of Christ (Reformers) from 1800-1840,* (B.D. Thesis, Butler University, 1936) pp. 13-15.

32. W. E. Garrison and A. T. DeGroot, *op. cit.*, p. 531.

33. C. Lockhart, "Ministerial Education," *The Christian Quarterly, New Series* (January, 1897), p. 72.

34. John A. Williams, *Life of Elder John Smith* (reprint), p. 95.

35. J. Challen, *Millennial Harbinger* (July, 1851), cf. p. 401. Also *Lard's Quarterly* (January, 1865), p. 223. And T. P. Haley, *New Christian Quarterly* (October, 1893), cf. pp. 429, 430.

36. B. Franklin, "Ministerial Education," *Millennial Harbinger* (January, 1864), p. 29.

37. *Millennial Harbinger,* (1856), p. 491.

38. *Christian Standard* (July 13, 1940), p. 670.

39. "Ministerial Education," *Lard's Quarterly* (April, 1865), p. 248.

40. J. J. Haley, *Makers and Molders of the Reformation Movement,* 1914 (College Press: Restoration Reprint Library, reprint ed.), p. 141.

41. "Schools for Preachers," *Gospel Advocate* (April, 1875), p. 346.

42. Earl I. West, *The Search for the Ancient Order,* Vol. 2, p. 124.

43. *Ibid.*, p. 301.

44. *Ibid.*, p. 305.

45. *Gospel Advocate* (August 16, 1877), p. 505.

46. *Ibid.* (June 13, 1891), p. 377.

47. *Ibid.* (June 6, 1901), p. 361.

48. *Ibid.,* p. 396.

49. *New Christian Quarterly* (July, 1893), p. 335.

50. R. B. Montgomery, *The Education of Ministers of Disciples of Christ* (St. Louis: Bethany Press, 1931), p. 86.

51. "The Disciples of Christ Today," *The Scroll* (October, 1935), p. 248.

52. *The Shane Quarterly* (July, 1943), p. 137.

53. "The Development of Ministerial Training Among the Disciples of Christ," *The Shane Quarterly* (July, 1943), p. 138.

54. "Do We Need a Theological School?" *Millennial Harbinger* (August, 1865), p. 365.

55. *Millennial Harbinger* (September, 1850), p. 512.

56. *The Shane Quarterly* (July, 1943), p. 141.

57. *Millennial Harbinger* (August, 1855), p. 474.

58. *Ibid.* (August, 1855), p. 538. Also E. L. Loos' article in *The New Christian Quarterly* (January, 1896).

59. *Ibid.* (September, 1855), p. 538.

60. T. P. Haley, "Our Ministry," *The New Christian Quarterly* (October, 1893), cf. pp. 429, 430.

61. *The Shane Quarterly* (July, 1943), pp. 142, 143.

62. Carroll C. Cotten, *The Imperative Is Leadership,* p. 61.

63. *Ibid.,* pp. 65 and 53.

64. W. E. Garrison and A. T. DeGroot, *op. cit.,* p. 417.

65. A. S. Johnson, *The Holy Spirit and the Human Mind* (Knoxville: Gaut-Ogden Co., 1903), p. 102.

66. *The Canton Christian* (September 6, 1929), p. 1.

67. *Christian Standard* (June 20, 1931), p. 611.

68. *Ibid.* (May 30, 1942), p. 532.

69. *Ibid.* (October 24, 1942), p. 1049.

70. *Ibid.* (September 26, 1953). See the editorial on p. 2.

71. W. E. Garrison and A. T. DeGroot, *op. cit.*, p. 417.

72. *Education for the Christian Ministry for Tomorrow's Church,* p. 8.

73. *Christian Standard* (January 9, 1954), p. 23.

74. *Ibid.* (June 21, 1941), p. 639.

75. *The Lookout* (December 29, 1974), p. 13.

76. *Christian Standard* (November 5, 1972), p. 3.

77. W. E. Garrison, *Heritage and Destiny,* p. 112.

78. *Christian Standard* (November 7, 1971), p. 22.

79. *Ibid.* (November 5, 1972), p. 25.

80. *Ibid.*

81. *Ibid.,* p. 26.

82. H. Adams, *Calling Men For the Ministry* (St. Louis: Bethany Press, 1945), p. 71.

83. *Millennial Harbinger* (October, 1865), p. 450.

84. "Bible School," *Gospel Advocate* (June 17, 1891), p. 377.

85. Daniel Sommer, "Notes and Annotations," *Octographic Review* (November 21, 1893), p. 1.

86. Leroy Garrett, personal correspondence, September 24, 1973.

support and placement

The Hirelings

Many writers have placed at Alexander Campbell's door the responsibility for the brotherhood's attitude toward ministerial salaries. B. L. Smith in his 1930 volume declared strongly:

> He made the ministry odious to many people. He was largely responsible for the lack of respect shown today to Protestant ministers. . . . There is something incongruous in a religious reformer's dying rich, while he had taught that other preachers should be kept in poverty.[1]

Campbell vowed never to receive any pay from his preaching; he "resolved never to receive any compensation for his labors."[2] Shortly after his declaration he was on the way to financial independence and did not have to test his pledge. However, he should be given the courtesy of his conviction.

The lasting influence from Campbell's pen was tte negative position he took in the *Christian Baptist.* No reader of the *Baptist* can avoid the impact of the poison-tipped barbs that this "clergy hunter" put to the bow in each issue. He had a passion to slay the "monied scheme of converting the world." However, from the beginning Campbell made a distinction between a "hireling priest" and a "preacher of the gospel." A preacher who was a true shepherd should have a shepherd's reward. He wrote in 1832, "I never did say that those who labored in the word and teaching ought not to be sustained by the brethren for whom they labored." The difficulty was that "some cannot" or were "unwilling to discriminate" between the man who "prepares himself for the office, learns the trade, and him who comes forward at the call and solicitation of the brethren."[3]

In volume 7 of the *Baptist* a reader inquired about preacher support in 1 Corinthians 9:14: "They which preach the gospel should live of the gospel." Campbell agreed to the principle, but he made a careful distinction between a traveling evangelist and a settled pastor.

> When also it becomes necessary for any Christian congregation, or congregations, to employ any of their qualified brethren to go

abroad and labor for the conversion of less favored neighbor-
hoods, . . . the New Testament . . . ordains that such should be
provided for, by the brethren who call them forth.

but there is no

command, example, hint, allusion (in the Bible) authorizing the
payment of an annual, monthly, weekly, or daily salary, to a man
hired to preach by the Sunday, one, twice, thrice, or four times in
the month, and during the six days work upon his farm. . . .[4]

**Campbell, more than generally realized, favored support for
area evangelists, supported by two or more congregations.
True *kerygma* deserved support. Weekly *didache* among the
brethren was a bishop's function and a gratuitous one at that.
Robert Richardson spoke of Campbell's thought in this area
in the early 1830's.**

As the few overtasked preachers already engaged were poorly
supported and wholly unable to supply the demands of the cause,
Mr. Campbell strongly urged that the churches should be arranged in districts, as he endeavored to show was the case in
primitive times, in order that, by mutual aid, they might sustain a
sufficient number of evangelists in the field.[5]

**This approach was not immediately successful. The satires in
the *Christian Baptist* against the "hireling" had taken their
toll. The liberality needed to sustain an effective evangelistic
ministry was not forthcoming.**

**There was a change in Campbell's accent on paying minis-
ters as he saw the brotherhood expanding and developing.
This can be illustrated by the following statements, made in
1829 and 1850 respectively:**

The overseers of christian congregations have a right by divine
appointment to a support from the brethren, whenever they call for
it. But still they are more worthy of honor, who do, as Paul coun-
seled the Ephesian Bishops, labor working with their own hands.[6]

and in 1850:

Better in some respects, that Paul had written a few more epistles
and manufactured a few less tents. Better he had demanded support from those whose duty it was, and who had the means, to
support him, and preached a little more. Better, I say, but for the
benefit of a noble example.[7]

Campbell realized in his later years that his earlier emphasis

could have been better placed. Yet he rarely had the fortitude to admit editorial errors of judgment. He was fascinated by Paul's self-support. Perhaps Alexander considered himself somewhat of a modern Paul.

Struggle for an Adequate Income

At the 1832 joining of Reformers and Christians the group sent out approved evangelists to tour the churches and explain the nature of the union. John Smith and John Rogers were selected as the first team. They were awarded the grandiose salary of $75 per quarter, or $300 per year.[8] Political salaries for this same year can be an interesting comparison. In 1832 President Andrew Jackson made $25,000 per year. John C. Calhoun, as Vice President, drew an annual salary of $5,000; and Edward Livingston made $6,000 as Secretary of State. However, the Attorney General drew only $3,500.[9] Today a cabinet official makes ten times what the Secretary of State did in 1832, while the average minister today makes twenty-seven times the salary commanded by Smith and Rogers. The ministry has climbed out of the pit of poverty.

Periodicals indicate that by 1840 many brotherhood preachers were in dire financial straits. Their distress signals were often considered pirate flags by congregations quoting Campbell's editorials against the hireling system. Samuel Rogers made a three-month preaching tour, and after paying expenses, netted less than enough to buy a new pair of boots. Against such a deplorable situation he wrote:

> Both among our preachers and people, there was prevalent a sense of foolish timidity upon the matters of taking up contributions of money for the ambassador of God, lest the world might conclude that he cared more for the fleece than he did for the flock. The little that we did receive was collected and given to us in a manner so sly and so secret, that the giver often appeared more like a felon than like God's cheerful giver.[10]

Isaac Errett perhaps had Campbell in mind when he wrote frankly of "prominent preachers" putting the people in an "injurious ease" by the false standard of gratis preaching. "There is enough for the wealthy preacher to do with his earnings, without leaving it to rust in the pockets of a too inactive brotherhood."[11] Barton Stone also wrote in favor of a ministry fully supported by the church, and deplored the necessity of a man having to work in secular employment to earn an adequate livelihood. But he was equally vocal against preachers becoming wealthy. His example was Jesus and the apostles; and it was enough for sincere men to "live in the style of those who send them."[12]

Since the middle of the nineteenth century many prominent men pleaded for more adequate financial confidence in the movement's ministry. Even Moses E. Lard could say in 1866 that "inveighing against the hireling system" had been "among the errors" of the restoration. This early emphasis "was unfortunate, and today we are still reaping the bitter fruits of it."[13] The congregations largely were of the opinion—at least expressed in their charity—that for a preacher poverty is an aid to piety.

Thomas Munnell was firm, in *The Care of All the Churches*, in making a church face its financial obligation to the preacher:

> To allow any member to escape paying his dues merely because he puts up some trifling excuse, or because he frequently puts it off, or finally insults the collector, shows that the officers are not prepared to have charge of the finances of the church.[14]

Arguing the point made by some churches that giving a preacher too much money would spoil him, Moses Lard retorted:

> You tell me it would cause him to neglect his calling. But how do you know this? You have never made one rich, to have the point tested.[15]

The independence of congregations has been a drawback to any uniform approach to increasing ministerial support. In 1928 a study of the income of 4,129 Disciples ministers showed an average salary of $2,217.[16] In 1949 the average income of some 3,500 members of the Pension Plan, which usually included a 15 percent salary allowance for a parsonage, was only $2,995.[17] A 1941 editorial in the *Christian Standard* urged the churches to "be fair with the preacher." The editor declared that it is "the *duty of the church* to see that he has enough upon which to live as he should." No congregation should "force the preacher to beg for more money."[18] By 1971, as reported by the Pension Fund Bulletin of March,

1972, the average income of a Disciples of Christ minister had risen to $8,075, with 768 ministers earning more than $10,800. In 1963, only 3.6 percent of Disciples ministers earned over $10,800. The 768 who did so in 1971 represented 21.4 percent. But by comparison the business administration graduate with a Bachelor's degree earned $8,604 in 1970; and the graduate with a Master's degree was making $12,528.[19] The ministry is paid even today at a going rate that is less than other professions requiring comparable education.

The brotherhood, though largely in the middle and upper-middle economic bracket in the past thirty years or so, is low in financial giving. An evaluation of the statistics of the segments of the movement during this period will show the progeny of the Campbell-Stone movement to be fifth or sixth in size among American Protestant bodies, and somewhere between twentieth and fortieth in per capita giving. Ministerial support has suffered in proportion.

The Disciples of Christ ministerial support should be at least as high as any other segment of the brotherhood. Carroll C. Cotten reports this situation for 1973:

> The second largest source of occupational stress for ministers is personal finances. The need for more money is a serious problem for 26 percent of the ministers. The major source of stress, however, is relative financial deprivation—the feeling that one's salary is too low in relation to that of members of the congregation, other clergy, or other professionals—rather than the actual salary level.[20]

This finding undoubtedly exists for all ministers and preachers in the Disciples heritage. At this stage of church awareness, we should not confuse dedication and sacrifice with meaningless privation. Voluntary sacrifices will always occur in the Christian ministry. Involuntary privation results in men leaving the ministry at an alarming rate. Financial insecurity is not conducive to preaching Christ's peace.

There is no national or unified office or effort among the churches of Christ and the Christian churches for the upgrading of ministerial support. Among the Restructured Disciples of Christ there is concerted national effort. At present there are overlapping programs and procedures in the Board of Higher Education; the Pension Fund and Department of

Ministry and Worship in the Division of Homeland Ministries. Their efforts are toward more unification under one overall administrative office.

In the early part of the twentieth century, in British churches of Christ, the General Evangelist Committee engaged men for service who were delegated primarily as itinerant evangelists. In these years the minister's salary was arranged by private negotiation between the man and the committee.

> In 1942 the first salary scale was published in the Year Book; and it has been frequently raised since. Further attempts to ensure better conditions for the ministers have been made by the Committee, e.g., in encouraging Churches to give the minister his rightful place in the life of the Church, and in ensuring that manses shall be of a standard suitable for the work and standing of the ministry.[21]

Growth of Ministerial Relief

Little organized retirement or relief for preachers was available during the entire nineteenth century. They were hardly paid enough to live on when actively serving congregations. Commencing about 1860, editorial pens began scratching against this deplorable situation. Moses Lard wrote that it was disgraceful to permit aged preachers to be forgotten, and embarrassing if their needs were alleviated by outright charity. His solution was to call these retired men back into the field for evangelistic meetings, and then give them a "nice offering." This was "more delicate and Christian" and did not wound a man "by thrusting money in his hand as a pauper."[22]

The Board of Ministerial Relief was organized by the national convention of the Disciples of Christ at Dallas, Texas, in October, 1895, and was legally incorporated in Indiana in 1897. The 1909 Centennial Convention Program declared, "The primary purpose of this Board is the care and support of our aged and disabled dependent preachers or their widows."[23] This board was supported by voluntary contributions from the churches, and this soon proved itself quite inadequate. In the beginning year, fifteen ministers received an annual average aid of $76. By 1920 the board had 274 members. The Pension Fund of the Disciples of Christ took the place of the board in 1928, and began financing the program by individuals contributing to a reserve fund. In 1931, 391 ministers were being helped in the average annual sum of $262. Things were not any better by 1940. That year, 1,075 members were receiving aid, but the average had dropped to $207.[24] A 1964 Pension Fund tract declared that 90 percent of the Disciples of Christ congregations were participating with a membership of 5,800. In 1968 the participating membership was 6,300, with more than 2,100 ministers receiving benefits.

The Pension Fund of the Disciples of Christ has sponsored a "Week of the Ministry" since the 1930's, encouraging the local exchange of pulpits for the exaltation of the ministry in general and the furtherance of the fund in particular. This agency deserves praise for its untiring efforts to lift the ministry in proper prestige. It currently provides financial benefits in three areas: death in active service, disability, and retirement. Thirteen percent of the base salary of the religious worker is the current dues. In the words of F. E. Smith, secretary of the Pension Fund in 1940, "It is a dignified and businesslike arrangement in keeping with the honor of the church and the good name of the ministry."[25]

The independence of the congregations affiliated with the Christian churches has prevented them from developing a fund as have the Disciples of Christ. Many ministers of the Christian churches are not aware that they are eligible for membership in the Pension Fund. Since the late 1950's several private groups have offered retirement benefits to this segment. In 1959, the *Christian Standard* carried an article-announcement of a new retirement plan "now in operation" that had been established "with mutual investment funds as its foundation." Covering all employees of Christian churches, it was directed by a "management committee," with the Union Bank and Trust Company of Los Angeles "acting as trustee." This plan under the chairmanship of Russell Barber required the congregation to "invest 10 percent of the amount of the base salary" of the Christian worker.[26] Also in this field is Christian Benefits, Inc. The summer and fall, 1972, issues of *Specialized Christian Services,* a quarterly publication under the directorship of Ralph McLean, announced a "group insurance program" established with John Hancock

Insurance Co. of Boston. The "Group Retirement program" is available through the Republic National Insurance Co. of Dallas. Also in the 1970's, a newer plan has been advertised and promoted, from the Alexander Co., of Indianapolis. The "Pension Trust, Church of Christ" of Mt. Vernon, Illinois, advertises in *A Directory of the Ministry.*

Ministerial Placement

The Home Mission Planning Council of the United Christian Missionary Society presented a plan of ministerial placement, as a result of a committee study authorized by the International Convention meeting at Denver in 1939. The June, 1940, issue of *World Call* described the placement of ministers seeking a change of location. The minister filled out a confidential "Minister's Information Blank" and sent it to the state secretary. This created a furor among the more conservative brethren of the Disciples of Christ. Aldes L. Webb wrote in the *Standard:*

> Should this scheme succeed, what was once a great communion of free churches of Christ will become just another bishop-bossed denomination. For this reason we stand up to say, "Hands Off the Ark!"[27]

Other voices were distressed that the "Blank" had no request for information concerning "beliefs or convictions." They considered this as failing to protect the churches against unworthy men who would exploit the people. There was also the protest that the system came full-blown from the bosom of Home Mission Planning Council, and was a self-appointed system that ignored the wishes of pastor and church.

Thirty-two years later the above conservative voices and some one million members formed into a fellowship of Christian churches, formally separated from the Disciples of Christ. The spring, 1972, issue of *Specialized Christian Services* announced a new service for churches—"Church Leadership Exchange." It was "designed and developed to assist church and agency personnel, as listed in *A Directory of the Ministry,* in locating or re-locating their respective ministries." This exchange would help churches "efficiently consider only those candidates whose qualifications match their needs and preferences." Everything will be "discreetly confidential." The summer and fall, 1972, issue of the *Services* "News and Notes" again stressed the exchange, describing it as a semi-computerized service which seeks to "match" positions and personnel. Through the use of "key sort cards, selections can be made on the basis of expressed preferences in regard to age, sex, geographical area, size of congregation and community, skills, training, family, experience, etc., without reference to names." Again, the winter, 1972-73, issue felt called upon to explain that "CLE is NOT a 'preacher' bureau. It is a semi-computerized *service.*"

To my knowledge, no protest to this placement service has appeared in any leading periodical serving Christian churches. There is little difference between this exchange and the 1940 placement service of the Home Mission Planning Council. No reference is made to giving expression of faith or belief, and the exchange came into being through a self-appointed agent. Yet, every fault or fallacy that may have attended the Disciples of Christ endeavor is inherent in this Christian churches service. The practical fact is that the Christian churches came to recognize in 1972 a need that the Disciples were aware of thirty years previously.

Ministerial placement was conducted on an "announcement" basis since the 1870's by periodicals such as the *Christian Standard*. Ads for churches seeking preachers and preachers seeking churches' pulpits were not uncommon. The parties contacted each other and then continued the negotiations on a personal basis. Even today the *Standard* has a feature "Our Exchange." An example as appearing in 1971: "New church in challenging area needs full time evangelist. Salary. Moving expenses will be paid. Contact:. . . ."[28] Drawbacks to such a nonsupervised activity are obvious in the areas of character traits, prior pastoral difficulties, availability of prospects, salary scales, and ministerial specialties.

For the past twenty years or so the state organizations of the Disciples of Christ have insisted that national agencies, colleges, and seminaries not recommend ministers in response to congregational inquiries, but channel these requests into the offices of the state "secretary" or "executive minister." The state secretaries, now regional ministers, argued that they were in a unique position to know the needs of churches and pastors. The practical result has been to place great power of appointment in the hands of these area leaders, and to limit the channels of inquiry open to the churches. Perhaps Colton was right many years ago when he penned, "Power will intoxicate the best hearts, as wine the strongest heads."

Congregations need help in choosing a minister and ministers need help in relocating their service. Which agency or office deserves the claim to "sole benevolent paternalism" toward the churches and ministers? Perhaps none in a society of free churches. Yet a system can be so loose and individualistic that ministerial liberty shifts to ministerial license. Hollis Turley, president of the Pension Fund, made a charge in 1961 that still has relevance.

> Pastorless churches do not constitute the whole problem. I know of men today adequately trained and deeply consecrated who are without churches in a day when we claim there is a shortage. We simply have not developed the techniques as yet for the placing of ministers, although we have made tremendous progress in this field.[29]

Some precautions have always been taken to protect the churches. Unfortunately, there have been shepherd-garbed wolves. The minutes of the 1850 State Convention of the Illinois Christian Churches illustrates an early procedure. One Richard Sanders was passing himself off as a "Disciples preacher." The convention announced:

> We view him in disorder, and his moral conduct such as to merit our disapprobation . . . unless he desist from preaching until duly authorized by the congregation of which he may be a member, that we shall consider it our bounden duty to make his true position known to the religious community through the medium of the religious periodicals.[30]

The periodicals were used to curtail the activities of self-styled spiritual leaders. See the report of a knife-carrying, family-deserting evangelist in the April, 1842 issue of the *Harbinger*.[31] This inquiry appeared in the 1832 *Evangelist:* "Please inform me of the character and standing of Bro. Harris; report says, he has left a wife and child behind him."

Walter Scott replied: "Dear Bro. Burton: In answer to your letter pray accept the following. Brother Harris is an unmarried person, who has sustained a most unblemished character in the church of Cincinnati."[32] There was a positive side to periodical usage. When Kentucky first began sending out state evangelists under the auspices of the 1840 state meeting, J. T. Johnson suggested that the evangelists carry letters of credit from a congregation, and that periodicals publish their names and the "fields of labor."

Samuel F. Pugh, in 1953, wrote an informative booklet, *How to Select and Call a Minister,* that was widely distributed among the Disciples of Christ. It gave guidance to the church from the time the minister resigned through the installation of the new one. This kind of service calls for the cooperation of the congregational leaders and requires an ever-recurring process of education.

The *ad interim* ministry has assumed prominence among the Disciples of Christ, and is used less often and less effectively among the churches of Christ and the Christian churches. Congregations are taking more time to investigate prospective ministers. In the *ad interim* work there is also a recognition of fulfilling a psychological need. When a minister leaves a church feelings—both positive and negative—are stirred. The *ad interim* man can serve as a coordinator of congregational energy. "He can often clear the church of situations that would be difficult for an incoming pastor to handle, allowing him to begin his pastorate free of otherwise embarrassing conditions."[33] This service has also filled a gap in the lives of ministers who are retired but not tired. It is a service that an older man's experience handles well, yet a duty that lacks the pressures of a full-time pastorate. This allows the retired minister to continue his sense of contribution to his brethren.

In Britain, since the 1930's, when a minister completes his training at Overdale College he usually serves a period as a "probationer" on the staff of the Home Missions Committee. This committee is appointed by and responsible to the Annual Conference. J. Leslie Colver, the General Secretary for many years, describes the placement procedures:

After a probationary period of at least two years he may be ordained to the full-time ministry and will normally be employed by the Committee for the rest of his years in the ministry. The Committee annually invites and reviews applications from the Churches for the services of the ministers, and after consultation with them, arranges where they will serve. Once a minister is placed with a Church to the mutual satisfaction of all concerned, he is likely to remain there for a number of years, until such time as he, or the Church, desires a change; or until a change appears to the Home Missions Committee to be desirable in the interests of the Churches as a whole.[34]

Replacement

Replacement of ministers deserves consideration along with placement. A 1953 survey among the Disciples of Christ indicated that twenty-eight out of thirty-three State Secretaries found "it difficult to secure adequately trained ministers."[35] During this same period this segment of the Movement was proclaiming a need for one thousand ministers. A statistical study was made under Dean Stephen J. England of the Graduate Seminary at Phillips University, covering the twenty-seven years of 1916-1942 inclusive. During this period 10,182 new names were added to the Disciples of Christ *Year Books,* but for the same time, 8,754 names disappeared. This gave the Brotherhood an average annual gain of only fifty-three ministers. In the twelve year period of 1930-1941 inclusive, 3,438 new names appeared, while 3,848 dropped out. Here was an overall loss of 410 ministers analyzed from another vantage point:

These men on the average served as ministers only four years and two months, and in this time served four churches each. One reason why we need to recruit so many men is that after they are recruited they serve so briefly. What does it profit the church to persuade a man to become a minister, if, after four years, he will be in some other occupation?[36]

There appears to be a direct relationship between short pastorates and the rapid rate at which men quit the ministry. There is no reason to doubt a similar ratio among the churches of Christ and the conservative Christian churches for the same period. Most of the churches identified later with the Christian churches were listed in the Disciples *Year Books* at this time. A lack of inner stability and security account for a great majority of these resignations. It stems from such sources as lack of higher education, frustration in being a spokesman for God, economic sacrifice, and faulty methods of recruitment. Perchance more mature enlistment procedures would lessen the two problems. Too often the criteria for the ordered ministry has been "the nice boy who should be a preacher." Ministers viewing their service as a life-time calling endure better whatever financial hardships occur.

The Dean England study shows that 64 percent of Disciples pastorates were of two years or less. The 1931 survey by R. B. Montgomery, considering 2,150 resident pastors, revealed that 55.1 percent were of two years duration or less. Undoubtedly the difference in the nature of these studies will account for most of the differences in the percentages. The point remains; a restlessness rampant among the ministers of the restoration movement.

These figures may not be entirely accurate for the segments of the movement in the last twenty years. Yet the turnover in the ministry today is much more than the exigencies indicate. In 1961 Hollis Turley could still call attention to "this alarming proportion of men who are leaving the ministry." An expanded idea of ministry, a deeper concept for the fellowship of the saints will alleviate much of the problem of ministerial replacement.

Wallace A. Ely, writing for *The Christian* in 1972, gave some practical considerations to enhance "long tenure for ministers." One such was the simple observation of the pastor to cease irritating the membership by nagging the "church's official family." Akin to this is the ability of the minister to treasure confidences.

> When a pastor is able to button up his lip and nail down his tongue he is adding time to his stay in a pastorate. Everything that his members tell him confidentially must be treated confidentially. Pastors that can be trusted with personal matters are the ones who are asked to stay on year after year.[37]

Stability in life-service will be enhanced by an increasing concept of association among the ministers. Since the creation of the Society for the Advancement of Continuing Education for Ministry (SACEM) in 1968 and the Academy of Parish Clergy (APC) in 1969, the national and regional authorities of the Disciples of Christ have recommended these organizations of "professionalization." They are not likely to serve many preachers or pastors with the churches of Christ and Christian churches. Yet there remains a need for a voluntary association of ministers that can champion competence and growth without the trappings of ecclesiastical authority. Information and education would be twin aims for such a district or state organization. There is no Biblical reason why such an association could not provide opportunities for continuing theological and administrative education through seminars and publications.

Notes to Chapter 7

1. B. L. Smith, *Alexander Campbell* (St. Louis: Bethany Press, 1930), pp. 146, 147.

2. R. Richardson, *Memoirs of Alexander Campbell,* Vol. I, p. 275.

3. *Millennial Harbinger* (August, 1832), p. 426. See D. E. Walker, *Adventuring For Christian Unity* (printed in England, 1935), p. 28.

4. *Christian Baptist,* Vol. VII (September, 1829), reprint, p. 36.

5. R. Richardson, *Memoirs of Alexander Campbell,* Vol. II, (reprint), p. 351.

6. *Christian Baptist* (September, 1829), p. 33.

7. *Millennial Harbinger* (September, 1850), p. 484.

8. *The Christian Messenger,* Vol. VI (September, 1832), p. 286.

9. *The Evangelist* (October 1, 1832), p. 240.

10. J. I. Rogers, ed., *Autobiography of Elder Samuel Rogers* (Cincinnati: Standard Publishing, 1880), p. 109.

11. *Millennial Harbinger* (September, 1856), p. 511. See C. L. Loos' article, *Ibid.,* (January, 1865), p. 33.

12. *Christian Messenger* (July, 1843), cf. p. 71. See also *Ibid.,* (September, 1843), p. 154.

13. *Lard's Quarterlh,* Vol. 2 (1866), p. 380.

14. T. Munnell, *The Care of All the Churches,* p. 47.

15. *Lard's Quarterly* (September, 1863), p. 37.

16. R. B. Montgomery, *The Education of Ministers of Disciples of Christ* (St. Louis: Bethany Press), p. 1931.

17. *International Convention Addresses and Reports, 1949,* cf. p. 20.

18. *Christian Standard* (August 23, 1941), p. 863.

19. *U. S. News and World Report* (March 15, 1972).

20. Carroll C. Cotten, *The Imperative Is Leadership,* p. 86.

21. J. Leslie Colver, "Organization," *Toward Christian Union,* James Gray, ed., (Union Committee of Churches of Christ, 1960), p. 58.

22. *Lard's Quarterly* (October, 1866), cf. p. 381.

23. *Program of the International Centennial of the Disciples of Christ,* (Christian Churches) 1909, p. 65.

24. W. E. Garrison and A. T. DeGroot, *The Disciples of Christ: A History,* cf. pp. 503, 504.

25. *Christian Standard* (September 9, 1940), p. 886.

26. *Christian Standard* (January 31, 1959), p. 61.

27. *Christian Standard* (October 5, 1940), p. 1001.

28. *Christian Standard* (August 22, 1971).

29. Hollis Lee Turley, address delivered Kansas City Assembly of the International Convention of Christian Churches (Disciples of Christ), October 4, 1961.

30. Daniel Bates, ed., *The Western Evangelist* (Mount Pleasant, Iowa: April, 1851 issue.

31. *Millennial Harbinger* (April, 1842), p. 191.

32. *The Evangelist* (October 1, 1832) reprint, (Cincinnati: The Harbinger Book Club), pp. 238, 239.

33. *The Christian-Evangelist* (October 7, 1953), p. 960.

34. J. Leslie Colver, "Organization," op. cit. p. 58.

35. *Education for the Christian Ministry for Tomorrow's Church* (Lexington, Ky.: The College of the Bible, 1953), p. 6.

36. S. J. England, "The Ministry For Life," *International Convention Address and Reports,* 1948), p. 171.

37. *The Christian* (June 11, 1972), p. 10.

8
pulpit and
personal ministry

The Pulpit of the Fathers

During the early years of the nineteenth century, the Stone movement engaged mainly in preaching while the Campbell group accented teaching in restoring the "ancient order." Also the Christian adherents were more emotional in the pulpit than were the Reformers. C. C. Ware described Stone's approach:

> Religion hedged with much form bored him—worse, it froze his soul. However, his emotionalism was not a fault in the wilderness where his life was given. There the people were emotional and Stone belonged to them. He spoke their language.[1]

Walter Scott expressed "Campbellite" theology in the pulpit, adding his view of Christology, producing a greater commitment to the preached Word. By the 1830's the movement was a preaching movement, it was a "current Reformation."

Stone and his associates ignored the doctrines of election and reprobation in proclaiming a "free salvation to all through the blood of the Lamb."[2] This kind of heart-felt expression encourages emotional and extemporaneous preaching. Sermons were extemporaneous, being carefully thought out, but preached without manuscript. Of the early leadership Stone and Scott set the precedent for vivid evangelistic pulpit work. Thomas Campbell gave the touch of the devotional; Alexander Campbell was the polemicist.

Alexander "usually talked in conversational style, with scarcely a gesture from the beginning to the end of his discourse."[3] Rev. A. Humphrey heard Campbell in Louisville in 1849 when the Reformer was sixty-one years old. His impression included:

> His enunciation is distinct, and, as he used no notes, his language is remarkably pure and select. In his delivery he has not much action, and but little of that fervid outpouring which characterizes Western and Southern eloquence.[4]

It was not uncommon for Campbell to preach an hour and a half to two hours, and hold the audience in a profound stillness. This was the response to his elucidating "great themes that run like rivers through all Scripture."[5] Studying constantly, he built a great storehouse of philosophy, theology, and history. This was evident in every address. Campbell avoided the "proof-text" method and preached the grand movements of the Bible, drawing on Scripture for illustration. Mentioning an 1811 address some thirty-one years later, Alexander remarked apologetically he had been among Pedobaptists, and thus, "in our mode of preaching and teaching more textuary and formal than we have since learned is either scriptural or advantageous to speaker or hearer."[6] Campbell felt scorn for the preachers who "have been so ingenious as to preach for twenty or thirty years without making anybody the wiser in the holy writings."[7] This was the fate of those who could not distinguish between "preaching the gospel" and "making sermons about the gospel." The differences were as great as between physicians who effect a cure of a disease and those who discourse on the nature of diseases. Thomas Munnell a quarter century later could expand this point:

> Beware of treating mere *subjects* as such, that may meet no want of the soul, that may lift no burden, comfort no heart, nor enlighten any mind on questions that lie in their way.[8]

Campbell's preaching was affected by two major influences. His Lockean philosophy of preaching left little if any room for direct revelation from the Holy Spirit. He was wont to say that the Bible is the "fountain and source of light and life." The second influence was from the Dutch theologian Johannes Cocceius, whose covenant theology affected the Seceder Presbyterians. Campbell's Calvinism was altered by this accent upon man's role in conversion. Cocceius stressed reasonableness of Scriptural interpretation and the suppression of interpretation of allegory and symbolism. D. S. Burnet presented an accurate evaluation of the Bethany Sage in his "Memorial Discourse" given one week after Campbell's death on March 4, 1866:

> As a *speaker*, I never knew him equalled in his peculiar sphere. He was not what the world calls an orator, and could not be

compared with J. N. Moffit, nor with the greater Whitefield. He had not Whitefield's voice—his action, nor his emotions, nor had Whitefield his mind, nor had he Wesley's enthusiasm and directness. He had feeble exhortatory power and he was seldom tender. The pathos of Kirwen he could not approach. But he drew crowds equal to either of the orators.

He was clear. He was generally understood by the masses, always by the cultivated. His entire mastery of the Bible captivated every one; all felt his power there.[9]

Walter Scott's preaching evidenced more systematic theology than Alexander Campbell's. Where Campbell's mind was analytical, Scott's was constructive and synthetic. Though evangelistic, Scott's sermons did not stop at the halfway house of exhortation and moralization. He appealed to the intellect as well as to the emotions. James Challen wrote of him that he had a "high strung nervous temperament," but there was a "loftiness and grandeur about him that struck the beholder with awe."[10] To Scott goes the major credit or blame of the movement's reputation of preaching a clear, rational plan of salvation: belief, repentance, baptism, remission of sins, gift of the Holy Spirit, and Christian living in the hope of eternal life. In 1827, Scott first linked baptism and forgiveness of sin. This became the dominant theme of baptism for a hundred years. Critics of the movement were quick to dub it "water salvation." Some present-day critics see this approach coming too near to a mechanical system that lacks the variability of the Spirit. They would eschew all tendencies toward legalism. And legalism did develop in many Disciples pulpits in the nineteenth century. It was inevitable in the war against the wild emotionalism and mysticism of much frontier preaching. J. J. Haley expressed it in 1914:

"First weakness" of the Disciples in their 19th century preaching was an "overplus of intellectualism." They conceived and interpreted religious truth in terms of the intellect, failing at first to perceive that this would lead them directly into the dogmatism and legalism from which they were trying to escape, and some of them have not perceived it yet.[11]

An example of Scott's preaching is in Volume I of the *Evangelist.* In "Sacred Colloquy" he speaks of sinners and sin in six concepts: the love, practice, state, guilt, power, and punishment of it. Applying the "gospel theory" to sinners:

Faith is to destroy the *love* of sin; repentance to destroy the *practice* of it; baptism the *state* of it; pardon to destroy the *guilt;* the spirit to destroy the *power;* and the resurrection to destroy the *punishment* of sin.[12]

Under the influence of Campbell, brotherhood preachers utilized the approach of "dispensational truth." The Scriptures were viewed as presenting an unfolding, ever-maturing revelation from God, culminating in the person of Jesus of Nazareth. W. T. Moore described it:

The Patriarchal, Jewish, and Christian dispensations are related to one another, but each has a place of its own, and the special function must be recognized, if we expect to understand the Bible.[13]

This belief undergirded the pulpit accent on rediscovering the New Testament church. A return to apostolic practices and views was held as prerequisite to achieving the spiritual results of apostolic times.

The impression must not be left that the great majority of restoration preachers were as self-contained as Campbell. As observed, the Christian preachers generally were more emotional and evangelistic than the Reformers. After the 1832 union, Reformers and Christians often went out in pairs as evangelists. "The Campbell man was the preacher who turned on the light, the Stone man was the exhorter who poured in the fire."[14] Aylett Rains and John Allen Gano were such a team. An old mountain man said to J. J. Haley toward the end of the nineteenth century, "Come and go on a preaching tour with me. You'll lighten and I'll thunder, and we'll bring 'em in."[15] The preacher spoke to the head; the exhorter thrust at the heart.

Sunday Is for Saints

The early nineteenth-century Reformation understood a distinction between *kerygma* and *didache.* Preaching seeks not merely to enlighten but to light up people. Preaching is more than having to face our problems, for it brings us face to face with God. Campbell saw a distinction between proclaiming the gospel and expounding Biblical truths. He therefore rejected the sermonic essay that was in vogue in many Prot-

estant pulpits. Thus one preached to unconverted sinners; one taught the saints. Campbell explained:

> The *preacher* singly aims at the conversion of his hearers, while the *teacher* intends the development of a passage, a doctrine, a theory; or in vindicating the tenets he has espoused. . . . The preacher aims at producing *faith* in his auditory; the teacher at imparting *knowledge* to his disciples.[16]

So the evangelist went out preaching, and the shepherd taught the flock. The idea of an itinerate preacher holding meetings in established churches was not in the definition of the early movement.

The present practice of churches of Christ and Christian churches (and formerly Disciples of Christ congregations) extending an "invitation" after each Sunday morning message is not an accurate portrayal of early Disciples' preaching. Those proclaimers were out where the people lived and worked, preaching to the unsaved. The present Sunday sermon has been called an "illusory substitute for preaching," for it preaches the gospel to the saved. William Moore evaluates the first-century worship message in relation to the Jewish synagogue procedures.

> The custom of delivering a sermon was carried over from the synagogue to the church just as were other formal features of the synagogue services, such as the prayers, the reading of the Hebrew scriptures, and the singing of psalms. The sermon in the church, like the regular discourse in a synagogue service, would be basically teaching *(didache).*[17]

Campbell held a similar view, believing that the *kerygma* was not a part of public worship of the primitive church. Thus what "preaching" was to be done came under the function of the bishop. Sunday was for saints. The evangelist gave the *kerygma* to the unsaved six days a week, and the eldership conducted worship on the Lord's Day. Campbell wrote in 1833:

> The system of sermonizing on a Text is now almost universally abandoned by all who intend that their hearers should understand the testimony of God. Orators and exhorters may select a word, a phrase, or a verse; but all who feed the flock of God with knowledge and understanding know this method is wholly absurd. Philosophical lectures upon a chapter are only a little better. The

discussion of any particular topic, such as faith, repentance, election, the Christian calling may sometimes be expedient; but in a congregation of Christians the reading and examining the different books in regular succession, every disciple having the volume in his hand, following up the connexion of things, examining parallel passages, . . . will do more in one year than is done in many on the plan of the popular meetings of the day.[18]

In this light, it is understandable that Campbell did not believe that preaching should hold the central place in a worship service. It would appear that many of the first generation brotherhood preachers did not accept his position. As the settled pastor system became more prominent, Campbell's concept received less attention and adherence. Campbell's approach is identified more today with the street preaching of the Salvation Army and the "storefront" churches and mission stations.

In 1853 Campbell delivered an address at the Kentucky state convention, in which he "strongly objected" to some churches "depending too much on itinerant preachers, and neglecting to call forth and employ the gifts of their own members in mutual exhortation and instruction."[19] He extolled a "proper eldership to teach and exhort from house to house and watch over the spiritual interest of the flock."[20] In the *Scheme of Redemption* Robert Milligan asks the question, "In what does the preaching of the Word consist?" He answers both negatively and positively:

1. It does not consist in preaching one's self.
2. It does not consist in the defense or advocacy of any party system.
3. It does not consist in the defense and demonstration of any system of science, literature or philosophy.
4. It does consist simply in preaching Jesus Christ and Him crucified.[21]

Today the general custom in most churches of Christ and Christian churches is to evangelize in Sunday worship services. Again, the rule would be to "offer the invitation" at the close of every public service. Assuming the validity of Campbell's interpretation, this kind of preaching would appear more logical for the nineteenth-century service where the unchurched comprised a larger portion of the audience.

The Disciples of Christ have accepted a more liturgical form and design of preaching. This approach does not produce a dichotomy between *kerygma* and *didache*. It has been expressed that proper liturgical preaching has three emphases derived from the New Testament: *kerygma,* preaching to the unconverted; *paraklesis,* a renewal and deepening of the *kerygma; didache,* the instruction of converts in doctrine and ethics.

There is a weight of truth that the brotherhood in this century has paid more attention to the *psychology* of worship than the *theology* of worship. More concern appears to have been given to the subjective experiences than to the objective disclosures. If Acts 2:42 is normative, worship in the early church consisted primarily of teaching, fellowship, the Supper ("breaking of bread"), and prayers. Perhaps the Disciples have been most negligent in "fellowship" and "teaching." Bernard Schalm, a Baptist college professor, has expressed this idea of worship: "Modern shepherds spend too much time mending fences and not enough time feeding the sheep." Having fallen victim to the lure of the topical and textual pulpit approach, the movement has failed to highlight doctrinal and "chapter" and "book" preaching. Congregational fellowship has too often been relegated to the "fellowship hour" after Sunday evening services. In our current American scene we tend to equate fellowship with action and interaction. Acts 2:42 contemplated fellowship in worship, not spectatorism. Unity in corporate worship, active participation in the elements of worship carries its own unique blessing. Isaac Errett wrote in his sermon, "The Fellowship," "We give the right hand of fellowship but it seems at times the left hand doesn't know what the right hand is doing."

God meets His people in the corporate prayers as well as during the Supper and the presentation of the spoken Word. A prophetic religion needs constant reevaluation, rededication and renewal. The vision for this community of faith is brought into focus by "the prayers." Prayers of adoration, confession, and submission feed the organism that is the church. Prayers of intercession probe for reconciliation. We do not become full-grown in His service the day after we are "born again." There is no instant sanctification, for we "work out our salvation with fear and trembling." Prayer provides a path. Sunday is for saints.

Preacher Styles and Habits

Pulpit decorum has taken a pleasant turn from the frontier days to the modern city or suburban church. Moses Lard, in 1865, asked young ministers to "refrain from spitting on the pulpit floor," though quickly adding that such a rebuke was "not intended to apply to old speakers whose habits . . . were formed before they entered the pulpit."[22] One such was Raccoon John Smith who liked to tap in a pinch of snuff after finishing his message. "Chawing and spittin' " was not the only personal habit of frontier preachers that might cause a raised eyebrow today. It was not uncommon for preachers to drink hard liquor, and it was not unusual for them to take a little "fortifying nip" at the beginning and end of a long ride on horseback. Corn liquor was a favorite, and peach brandy was popular in Kentucky, Tennessee, and Georgia. At the close of the frontier and the turn into the twentieth century, the acceptable behavior of the minister took on more strict dimensions. Morris Butler Book spoke for the great majority of the conservative elements when he said in 1941:

> The preacher who frequents the dance hall, who deals out a deck of playing cards, who smokes or chews or peddles dirty jokes has not only repudiated the very honor of his calling, but he has disgraced the cause of Christ.[23]

Book added, "A hawk is not a flamingo just because it has feathers." Certain pulpit decorum in the early and middle nineteenth century would not pass inspection in any brotherhood congregation today. Docile congregations were an exception, and John Smith could say with experience that honey could be used to capture flies, but "if attacked by hornets use vinegar." Smith, in the late 1820's, so reports his biographer J. A. Williams, was making heavy inroads into a Calvinistic community. One day he greeted a man, "Good morning, brother."

He replied, "Don't call me brother. I would rather claim kin with the devil himself."

Said Smith, "Go then and honor thy father!"[24]

On other occasions when one would rise to leave during his sermon, John Smith would shout, "The wicked flee when no man pursueth." This usually kept the timid soul in the pew. Activity in the pulpit was deemed by many to be beneficial to the message. However, "body English" did not noticeably improve the King's English. President Lincoln likened much frontier preaching to "a man fighting bees." Alexander Campbell, in a bit of satire stated in the *Christian Baptist:*

> In this holy paroxysm of clapping, rubbing, sneezing, and roaring, the mind is fairly on the way, and the tongue in full gallop, which, like a race horse, runs the swifter the less weight it carries.[25]

Campbell's decorum was more breached than emulated. An animated audience made it easy for a preacher to dramatize his message.

The length of sermons in any era may be indicative of its relative importance and worth to worship. The early Reformers thought nothing of preaching two to three hours at a standing. At the scene of their immersion, Thomas and Alexander Campbell preached a "double header" that lasted nearly seven hours.[26] Raccoon Smith on occasion would spent an hour on each section of a three-part sermon. He preferred such a division; "In the first he corrected misrepresentations; in the second, he expressed popular errors; and in the third, he presented the simple Gospel to the people."[27] Moses Lard indicated in his *Quarterly* that his average time in the pulpit was one and a quarter hours. It would not be inaccurate to estimate the average sermon length at one hour in the middle nineteenth century. Thomas Munnell, being a little more pew conscious, suggested an occasional twenty-five to thirty minute sermon. "A gentle surprise might be healthy occasionally."

Until the turn of the twentieth century, the sermon and the Lord's Supper accounted for the greater part of the worship service. In 1918, W. T. Moore complained that the psychology of the twelve o'clock "mental dinner bell" was cutting the sermon time to a disgraceful thirty minutes. Such a practice made it "impossible" for ministers to "preach great sermons even when they are abundantly able."[28] It is just as well that Moore is not surveying the current worship scene where pastors count themselves fortunate if there are twenty-five minutes left after announcements, business, songs, and solos. Perhaps a wise and skillful minister today can learn to express in twenty-five minutes a gospel message that had fifty minutes allotted to it in a prior generation. The present world's timetable would not permit a two-hour sermon. The congregation would not sit still that long. Many of the old churches in Sweden, Scotland, and on the Continent had an hourglass sitting on the pulpit. It would take a bold prophet today to complete his hour and turn the glass over for a second go.

Preaching was a form of spiritual combat on the frontier. Often preaching in the formative period of the movement was in the mold of theological warfare, in which the combatants and the spectators all knew the rules. The actions used by Raccoon Smith in getting and holding an audience's attention were analogous to the proverbial farmer with the board getting the attention of the mule. But what lesser lights were unable to control, Campbell, Scott, Creath, Smith, Johnson, Franklin, Lard, and others handled adroitly and fashioned admirably in the matter of pulpit and pen controversy. Today, more so in the ranks of the churches of Christ, some preachers still see in debate and confrontation the key to the kingdom. The concensus is against them. The role of the minister today has been expanded to such an extent that no longer is "swinging the staff" considered mature "sheep tending." In the area of psychology of personality it is rare to find in a minister the composite of the wolf and the lamb, the warrior and the shepherd, the exposer and the composer. Yet, Biblical preaching need not be dull or damaging. Biblical preaching should be for challenge and commitment, growth and service.

In a friendly spirit of advice Moses Lard described a mature pulpit style, which often escaped his own adaptation:

> Let him who sets out to preach, early learn this lesson, that man has a heart as well as a head. Logic is for this, love and sympathy for that. . . . Logic merely cracks nuts, but love and sympathy unseal fountains of kindness; and few men, after all are so lost as to be wholly devoid of the latter.[29]

Today, in preparation for an M.Div. or D.Min. degree from a Disciples of Christ seminary, a student is expected to study and absorb techniques in church administration and finance. In a church of Christ college, such studies are deemed unnecessary, if not frivolous, for the education of an evangelist. G. H. P. Showalter's presentation at the Abilene Bible lectures in 1944 is typical. He stressed that a preacher should be a fighter for the Lord, not a businessman. Preachers must be careful not to be "a meddler in other men's matters." The conclusion was that it is "inexcusable and unendurable for one in the position of a local evangelist to be thus ensnared."[30] Even when a preacher considers himself as the shepherd of the flock, his theology of pastoring may be circumscribed so that he feels responsible for "spiritual" leadership only. Many ministers of Christian churches and the preachers and evangelists of the churches of Christ accept the position that the Bible preacher is not to be thought of as a church executive or a promoter. He primarily gives verbal witness to the Word. These ministers would agree with Lynn Gardner that "forceful public preaching of Christ has always been central when the church was on the evangelistic move."[31]

Priscillas In the Pulpit

Little doubt exists as to the opinion of the restoration early leaders concerning "women preachers." The liberal-hearted Barton Stone was "seriously led to conclude by the Scriptures" that "women are excluded from taking part in any judiciary matters of the church." Such would be "derogatory to the government established by infinite wisdom."[32] There was general concensus on this point. In 1840 an Ohio reader of the *Harbinger,* signing himself "J.C.A.," asked Alexander Campbell: "Have the sisters a right to teach? If so, Who? When? Where? In other words, have the sisters a right to deliver lectures, exhortations, and prayers in the public assembly of the church of God?" Campbell's reply was short, emphatic, and final: "Paul says: 'I suffer not a woman to teach, nor to usurp authority over the man; but to learn in silence' (1 Timothy 2:12). I submit to Paul, and teach the same lesson."[33] Seventeen years later in answer to another Ohioan's questions concerning women's leadership in worship, he pronounced:

As to sisters in Christ's family Paul has decided that they should *learn* in the church. . . . The Lord has not commissioned women to take any precedence over men. As for singing and praying they are equal in all the public acts of devotion—as far as *communion* is concerned; but in taking the lead or precedency in any of these in the Christian assemblies is not allowed by Paul. His judgment in this matter is paramount and final.[34]

The conservative J. W. McGarvey was sure that Phoebe was not a deaconess, but only a "servant" of the church at Cenchrea (Romans 16:1). He was a little upset by the growing responsibility women were assuming as church leaders. He believed that women should not "be ambitious for offices and especially for offices unknown to the apostles."[35] McGarvey allowed women to attend his classes at the College of the Bible, provided they abided by certain restrictions and procedures. Mrs. Justine Weaver recalled her experiences in 1895 when Brother McGarvey required that "she sit on the back seat, next to the door," and at the close of the lecture "when I nod my head to her, she arise at once and leave the room before I dismiss my class," and on days of "questionable text she quietly withdraws, before the class begins."[36] McGarvey was sure that after any female studied the Scriptures with him she would "learn that women are not to be preachers."[37] It was his firm position that Christ refused to have any woman speak in the churches as teachers of men.

Very few Disciples ministers or leaders spoke in favor of women "evangelists" or "missionaries" before 1865. Yet, the movement was concerned with female education and added its share of "female seminaries" to the national growth of such institutions. Claude Spencer, curator of the Historical Society, has found records of more than forty such educational ventures operated by the Disciples prior to 1865.

The general opinion of the great majority of brotherhood leaders in the nineteenth century was that Paul's admonition in 1 Corinthians and 1 Timothy was binding upon the church as to woman's role as congregational teacher or preacher, elder or evangelist. It was often stated that only a "naturally insubordinate woman" would take offense at Paul's words. Thus Christian women who had the traits of "modesty, humility, and submissiveness" would recognize the truth of these

Scriptures. W. K. Pendleton would quote Tertullian to show that in the Montanist movement of the second century those advocating female preaching were "heretical women." The few voices advocating an increased role for women were often lumped with the revolutionary and radical political elements.

In the middle and late nineteenth century men like Isaac Errett, J. H. Garrison, W. T. Moore, and Thomas Munnell advocated a greater place of responsibility for women in church work, but not in the pulpit. Moore cautioned that women are not "in their true position when they go into the pulpit," except for "special occasions." He did not want to make a Scriptural issue of his opinion, preferring to think of it "from the point of view of the appropriate." A woman "must be womanly" if she expects to exert the best influence.[38]

Elizabeth Ann Hartsfield, treasurer of the College of the Bible, believes that three things contributed to the opening of worship opportunities to women: women entered industry and gained economic freedom; they attended schools of higher learning and assumed new areas of responsibility; and then assumed leadership necessary in the churches due to the man-shortage during the War Between the States.[39] The literary field was opened by a series of articles in *The Apostolic Guide* in 1886 by a lady (Miss or Mrs.?) using the signature M.R. Lemert. She claimed four score years, and declared in one essay:

> The doctrine that seals woman's lips in the church assembled—that affirms that Paul (1 Cor. 14:34-36) prohibits the free religious use of women's tongue is a heresy—a *mere assumption* involving consequences dire. It impeaches the wisdom of God. It accuses him of acting in bad faith with women—of mocking her. It also impeaches Paul—accused him of transcending his mission; of contradicting himself—pulling down what he has built up—in short, of committing moral suicide.[40]

The organizational field blossomed with the formation of the Christian Woman's Board of Missions at the General Missionary Convention in Cincinnati, in October, 1874, under the leadership of Mrs. C. N. Pearre. Thomas Munnell and Isaac Errett were to give much moral and literary support to the organized work of the Disciples women, yet they could not encourage women to preach. In the last quarter of the nineteenth century a few women did reach the podium and did receive the title of "preacher." It is reported that Melissa Garrett Timmons Terrell, born 1834, was ordained in 1867 in Ohio by the Deer Creek Conference of the Christian church. J. F. Burnet records:

> Mrs. Terrell was the first woman ordained by the Christians, and probably the first in modern times to be ordained by any denomination by direct authority of a Conference or local congregation.[41]

Mrs. Terrell may well have been the first woman ordained among the Disciples. Ellen Moore was the first to receive a B.D. degree, graduating from the College of the Bible in 1916. The *Christian-Evangelist* (December 31, 1925) carried the obituary of Clara Celestea Hale-Babcock, born 1850 in Ohio, who was ordained to the ministry in 1888 and served as pastor of churches in Illinois and North Dakota. She is credited with some 1,502 baptisms. Another early Disciples woman preacher was Sara McCoy Crank, born 1863 and ordained 1892. Her husband, J. R. Crank, was also a preacher. She was ordained by J. S. Clements, general evangelist for the American Christian Missionary Society. When the Cranks moved to Paragould, Arkansas, in 1906, the church board forbade her to preach. She pitched a tent nearby and held a revival meeting.[42] The *Christian-Evangelist* (November 24, 1948) carried her obituary, and the writeup credited to her ministry more than one thousand funerals, 761 weddings, and more than five thousand baptisms.

In 1973 *The Christian* carried a weekly series on ordained women in the ministry. In the August 12, 1973, issue Cassie D. Livingstone, now ninety-two and retired, stated she attended Charles City College in Iowa, was ordained in Concord, Illinois, in 1905, and retired in 1950. She served churches in Iowa, Illinois, Kansas, and Oregon. Rebecca Jane Bunton, another lady pastor in this series, who received her seminary training at Christian Theological Seminary, indicated the problem of acceptance at this period among the Disciples of Christ when she penned: "I have a concern for the Church's other women who are seeking to be accepted as pastors and ministers with full status.[43]

In 1952 the General Department of United Church Women

reported that the Disciples of Christ had 39 pastors among some 298 ordained women. At the same time the American Baptist reported 33 women preachers and the Congregational Church noted 81. The 1953 *Year Book* of the Disciples of Christ listed 442 women in the "Ministers' Directory." One hundred ninety-five were missionaries or retired missionaries; 87 were in general administrative work; 42 were pastors; 35 preached occasionally; 9 were in business, but preaching occasionally; and 28 listed themselves as evangelists. Thus 114 women could be classified as fairly regular in pulpit work. As a percentage figure among the 7,801 names in the directory, only 1.4 percent are women preachers. A comparison with the directory of the 1970-1971 *Year Book* is interesting. It lists 6,970 Disciples of Christ ministers, of whom 2,737 were pastors of local congregations, and 1,131 were retired but preaching. Four hundred forty-five women were included in these categories: 150 retired; 71 Christian education; 32 in business, but preaching; and 17 pastors of local congregations. Seventeen out of 2,737 pastors is a percentage of .6 percent. This same year, 1970, 28 Disciples of Christ women were enrolled in Disciples seminaries—5.6 percent of all Disciples enrolled. The trend is definitely upward.

In 1957 Samuel F. Pugh, national director of church development of UCMS, produced a booklet, *Women's Place in the Total Church.* His "Introduction" included the following: "The author is in favor of having women as voting members on every church board. Leaders in the church should be chosen on the basis of ability rather than sex."[44] Mr. Pugh believed women should serve in church leadership because women are more aware of children's needs, "more adept at detail," have an eye for good housekeeping, and lend dignity and harmony to meetings.[45]

The present Disciples of Christ position on women in the ministry, as represented by the occasional writings of such national leaders as J. Daniel Joyce, former dean of the Graduate Seminary at Phillips University, and Chester A. Sellars, retired area minister and feature writer for *The Christian,* would find agreement with the statement made in 1954 by Howard E. Short, then professor at the College of the Bible:

Their (Disciples of Christ) belief in the priesthood of all believers must include a recognition of women in any service of the church. . . . Woman's place in the service of the church is a matter to be determined upon sociological and psychological grounds, rather than upon theological grounds. This is the only way that the various references to women in the Bible, especially in Paul's writings, can have any meaning when taken as a whole.[46]

The current Disciples of Christ position is to accent Galatians 3:28, "there is neither male nor female, for you are all one in Christ Jesus," as the solution to ministerial attainment for women. They generally feel that women have suffered many indignities at the hands of the Biblical literalists. It is commonly held that 1 Corinthians 14:34, 35 is misplaced in the text, and perhaps is a later addition of an anti-feminist. Thus church leadership should be based on ability not sex. Women, last at the cross and first at the tomb, should have an essential role in the ongoing of the life of the church. In the last quarter century national Disciples of Christ women leaders have included Mrs. James D. Wyker, president of United Church Women of the National Council of Churches; Jessie M. Trout, vice-president of UCMS; Mrs. Marguerite Harmon Bro, noted writer and educator; Mrs. Forrest Richeson and Mrs. Alec J. Langford of the Christian Women's Fellowship.

The churches of Christ continue to hold the position of the early nineteenth-century leadership on women preachers. This approach is uniform for women leadership in general. Deaconesses are virtually unknown. A woman elder is unthinkable and pagan in origin. A woman preacher would be heresy. The statement of Winthrop H. Hopson, noted Missouri preacher of more than a century ago would speak for the non-instrumental brethren today:

Educated, protected, honored, loved, what more could she ask. Would she yield the gentle voice of supplication and persuasion for the boisterousness of command? . . . Would she at one fell stroke destroy the sacred altar, at which man has ever knelt with an adoration that stops but little short of idolatry? . . . No, no! if she be wise.[47]

Where Disciples of Christ leadership would accent sociological, psychological, and philosophical grounds in justifying a female ministry and administrative leadership, the churches of Christ are only concerned with literal, Biblical qualifications for such service. There really is nothing to discuss. First Timothy 3:1-13 and Titus 1:5-9 clearly state that the "bishop" and the "elder" shall be the "husband of one wife." This can only mean an exclusive male eldership, and by analogy male evangelists.

No ordination procedure is available among the non-instrumental segment and no regional, national, or educational authority that can recognize ministerial standing. Private correspondence from Leroy Garrett in 1973 expressed the procedure:

> It is tantamount to 'ordination' to graduate from one of our schools and be accepted by a congregation as a minister. Even this college background is not necessary. . . . This is measured mostly by one's ability to be accepted as a minister. If *he* is a preacher, then *he's* a preacher (emphasis mine).

All ministers and missionaries are recognized and controlled by the eldership of a local congregation. This all-male eldership is quite unlikely to accept a female preacher or evangelist. The churches of Christ would view as a complete *non sequitur* the statement by Chester A. Sellars in *The Christian.* "The congregation should very carefully select men and *women* who meet the *scriptural* qualifications of elder" (emphasis mine).[48]

Christian churches would generally approve the 1971 statement by Noble Tribble in his column in *The Lookout:*

> There are many women teachers mentioned in the Bible, but no women evangelists (ministers). Therefore, we must conclude that the Lord wanted women to teach but not to preach.[49]

Some Christian churches do appoint women as deaconesses to direct the women's work of the church, visit sick and shut-ins, prepare Communion for the Lord's Supper, and assist in the missionary endeavors. Rarely would they serve the Supper, and they are universally excluded from the eldership. Contrary to the position of the churches of Christ, women are adult as well as children teachers in the Bible schools.

Galatians 3:28 is interpreted as reference to the blessings and promises of the gospel, not to equal authority. The equal entrance into the kingdom is not a denial of sex or a magical removal of fundamental sexual characteristics. Thus Christian churches do not see this Scripture as having any bearing on church order. W. R. Walker expressed the basic outlook when he penned in 1938:

> Not one woman was invited to serve in the capacity of public minister as an apostle or preacher of the Word. That can not be explained as an oversight nor as a diplomatic concession to the social customs of the age.[50]

In the Bible colleges, year after year, women outnumber men in the freshman classes. The numerical advantage decreases as the students advance. Few women are in the graduate seminaries. The percentage of women who graduate from Bible college and go on to graduate studies has not been accurately evaluated for this segment of the movement. A 1972 study reported in Cincinnati Bible Seminary *Forum* for August indicated percentages for all graduates. "Enrollment in the graduate schools indicates that one Bible college student in three will go on to further classwork."

James D. Murch writing in his column "Today in Christendom" for the *Christian Standard* devoted an issue in 1971 to the role of women in the church. He notes the activity of women in the Scripture, believing more women would have been featured were it not for "the influence of the societal patterns of the day." He concludes:

> It seems to me that the time has come for the Christian community to re-examine all the Scriptures clearly with women's role in the church, and that it prayerfully consider the possibility of utilizing to an increasing degree those qualities of spiritually mature and capable women which fit them for church leadership and service.[51]

In the first century the Hebrew and the pagan priesthoods were entirely male. This has undoubtedly influenced the Roman Catholic Church in its tradition of reserving the priestly functions for men. In the primitive church, however, we find Priscilla (Acts 18:26) instructing Apollos. We do not know whether her teaching ministry was public or private. The four daughters of Philip "prophesied" (Acts 21:9). Again, we are not informed if this included congregational teaching or expounding of the Word in public worship. Other passages of Scripture that imply ministerial office for women have never received adequate evaluation from the conservative and fundamental segments of the brotherhood. These would include: Romans 16:1 (Phoebe is called a *diakonon);* Romans 16:3; 1 Corinthians 1:11 (Chloe); 1 Corinthians 11:5-16; 16:19; Acts 16:14, 15 (Lydia); 1 Timothy 5:2 ("the women" following qualifications for elders and deacons); 1 Timothy 5:3 (the "widows"). According to Romans 16, Mary "worked hard" in the church, Tryphena and Tryphosa are called "workers in the Lord."

Polycarp reports deaconesses in the second-century church. An order of deaconesses assisted the bishop at Holy Communion for centuries in the Eastern Orthodox Church. Miriam Y. Holden states:

> The latter half of the fourth century and the first half of the fifth century is the period during which the female deaconate of the East appears to have attained its highest importance. All the leading church writers of that period refer to it, such as Basil, Gregory of Nyssa, Chrysostom, Theodoret, and individual deaconesses are frequently mentioned in the church annals. However, the Council of Laodicea in 365 A.D. dismissed women from the ministry and forbade her to serve at the altar, while the Council of Orleans in 511 A.D. shut her out of the deaconate. A Synod at Orange in 441 had forbidden the ordination of deaconesses. In 517 the Council of Epaone in Burgundy forbade the imposition of hands upon women. . . . The restrictions on women deaconesses became more severe, and the Council of Auxerre, in 587 A.D., in a clearly discriminatory decree forbade them to receive the sacrament in their bare hands on account of their impurity and inherent wickedness.[52]

Luther and Calvin continued the theological outlook concerning the role of women in leadership that was current in their day. Neither saw any necessity for women to hold office in the church. Neither thought it Scriptural for women "to rule over men." Of course, women should minister to the needy and poor. And Luther did recognize that women could preach when out of necessity and "no man is available." He would not deny that there could be validity in the special activities of a prophetess.

In recent times the Quakers, with their open concept of the

ministry, have practiced a policy of equality between the sexes. Rufus Jones comments:

About the last thing any self respecting Englishman of the seventeenth century would have dreamed of would have been such a radical reconstruction of the Christian Church as to put women on precisely the same level as men, and to wipe out all sex distinctions in matters of religion. Just this innovation the Quakers actually made.[53]

The Prophetic Pulpit

David N. Suttren saw the minister as God's man of courage.

Opinions are ideas that men hold, but convictions are ideas that hold men. Great ideals, great ideas, eternal principles— convictions based on these principles are the hands of God by which he holds men and makes them brave.[54]

Prophetic preaching would be a courageous portrayal of the Christ of the Scriptures. But the prophetic role does not please everyone. Goettingen remarked more than one hundred years ago, "It is almost impossible to carry the torch of truth through a crowd without singeing somebody's beard." When strong preaching singes elders' or leaders' beards, there usually is kindled another fire or two. These flash fires have scorched many a preacher and a congregation among all denominations.

Historically, the Disciples have stressed prophetic preaching. Since the 1950's the Disciples of Christ have increased their emphasis on a social relationship, being guided by the social action department of UCMS. The national pronouncements of this department and the annual resolutions promulgated by the International Convention have exhibited what is identified as liberalism. This social emphasis has taken form in such fields as labor disputes, immigration laws, racial strife, amnesty for military deserters. These political emphases have produced new tensions in the Disciples of Christ between the professional ministry and the laity. Carroll C. Cotten has expressed it: "Ministers tend to view their role as leading and equipping the laity for their ministry to the world. Laity tend to view the minister as *their chaplain,* employed to preach, teach and comfort them."[55] Currently the regional and national leadership of this segment is accenting the pastor's responsibility to effect change in his community.

This emphasis on social change, as contrasted to the preaching of a personal gospel, has produced greater stress upon the Disciples of Christ minister than his pastoral counterpart in the other segments of the brotherhood. At state, regional, and national meetings, through publications and journals, there have been increased discussions of the insecurity of the Disciples of Christ pastor. This insecurity is usually related to the local leadership. The practical situation is buttressed by the 1971 study of Edgar W. Mills and John P. Koval, *Stress in the Ministry*.[56] This report supplies the data that of the ministers surveyed 75 percent reported frequent "highs" of stress. This was seen as stemming primarily from personal or idealogical conflict with parishioners. "Restructure" has been heralded as eliminating areas of such stress in "professionalizing" the ministry. This would be accomplished partly by the control of ordination and pulpit placement at the regional level and the expanded programs at the regional and national levels.

The Disciples began with a strong pulpit, and the early decades of denouncing creedal abuses and synodical authority put an outspoken fearlessness in their sermons. Preaching the Christ of the Scriptures was the heart of every message. It was a serious commission. Ben Franklin gave this advice for presenting the gospel:

> We want nothing sensational, no tricks, no comic performance; no private maneuvering to induce anyone to promise, "If you will join, I will"; no artifice to get around the people, come on them suddenly and surprise them. Come directly to the people from the start, and let them know what you mean, and work directly to the point—the enlightenment and salvation of men.[57]

Many of the frontier preachers had little formal education, and less training in pulpit presentation and speech. Franklin was one. In one of his early sermons a friend counted his use of "dear friends and brethering" 150 times. That is somewhat monotonous even for a ninety-minute sermon.

The early pulpit presentations were usually without notes or manuscript. Scripture was often given verbatim without looking at the Bible. This facilitated an extemporaneous approach that lent itself to the prophetic mood. This mood was largely in the lineage of Amos and Jeremiah for the nineteenth century. Denunciation was prominent in many quarters. Dwight E. Stevenson addressed this condition:

> Disciples sermons of the 1830's are different in kind from those of the 1960's, not simply because of what they are in themselves, but also—and more especially—because of the relation they bear to their cultural environment.[58]

In this period we find a dearth of pastoral preaching. Few devotional works were produced. The earliest ones include Robert Richard's *Communings in the Sanctuary* (1872), and Isaac Errett's *Walks About Jerusalem* (1871) and *Talks to Bereans* (1872). Many of the more bombastic brethren wondered if these preachers had lost their moorings and drifted out into the sea of mysticism. J. H. Garrison received greater acceptance with his 1891 volume, *Alone With God.*

The tendency of the evangelists such as Walter Scott, Ben Franklin, Moses Lard, J. T. Johnson, Raccoon Smith, Tolbert Fanning, and John F. Rowe was to deliver the same discourse over and over in different locales. These messages of ninety minutes or more were developed and polished works. J. W. McGarvey said of Moses Lard: "The number of discourses which he had elaborated to his own satisfaction was small, and he had no hesitation about repeating some of them a number of times at short intervals before the same audience."[59] McGarvey remembered one occasion before a Lexington audience when Lard announced a sermon that he had preached four times previously in the same house within two years. Upon seeing some looks of consternation, Lard is reported to have said, "It has taken me after many trials twenty years to bring it up to my satisfaction. I don't think that many of you can learn all that is in it by hearing it only five times."[60] These were largely doctrinal messages. The frontier pulpiteers were in accord with the view of Phillips Brooks that "no preaching ever had any strong power that was not the preaching of doctrine." It took a receptive man not to acquire a spirit of a sectarian while fighting sectarianism. The turn of the twentieth century was proof that not all Disciples preaching retained its prophetic content.

Prophetic preaching rests soundly upon serious preaching. There is authority in Christian solemnity. Alexander Campbell believed that "gravity" of this sort "gives to the messages of truth a passport to the conscience and to the heart" that otherwise would be denied vista. Traditionally, Disciples have not sought to dispossess the demons with a smile. Tom C. Brown wrote in the *Gospel Advocate:*

> Humor has its place in the pulpit, but there is a very small place. The preaching of God's word is, after all, a very serious matter. . . . Humor should be the "salt" and "pepper" used by the preacher to help emphasize, motivate and inform. It should not be the whole diet.[61]

The preacher in his finer role becomes a symbolic figure for the congregation, representative of the Word. Thus it is occasionally said and more often thought that the "ministry of the Word" is superior to the "ministry of the ordinances." Perhaps they are kept in proper balance by the "ministry of committed love."

P. C. MacFarland, then a California pastor, in the 1906 *Christian-Evangelist,* encouraged personal warmth in the pulpit. To him Jesus did not write books because the "true prophet and his message are one." In a sense Jesus wrote always—His actions being His Gospel "writ large." The complete preacher, the true prophet, must also be the pastor. There is the Hosea side to prophecy. Pointing the way is not enough, he must lead his sheep, or the choicest of words may be wasted. Tympanic religious vocalization is not gospel preaching. Lee Carter Maynard has observed, "it is easy to love to preach, without loving the sheep."[62]

Preaching power is not derived from graceful gesture, nor flowering language, nor glowing argumentation, nor novel and striking illustration. Perry Gresham has said:

> The difference between good advice and Christian preaching is in the depth, the authority, and the power to perform. It is the awful gulf between the word of God and the word of man.[63]

But there always lurks a danger, so easily camouflaged, of the man overshadowing the message by standing in front of the cross. More than 125 years ago Frederick Robertson cautioned, "Point to Jesus Christ and then get out of the way." Perry Gresham reminds us that some of the brethren read 2 Timothy 2:15 entirely too slowly, seeming to pause after "Study to show thyself . . ." James D. Murch's answer to this salient sin is for the minister to "come to his pulpit conscious that he is the ambassador of God to His people."[64] J. Clyde Wheeler presented the preacher as "God's spokesman" as long as he kept the pulpit as the church's "high place." He felt that the minister possesses his pulpit "just as long and as much as a courageous, daring, driving, alluring, divine spirit possesses him."[65] The pulpit will remain prophetic for our people as long as our total allegiance is to the Christ of the Scriptures, and we understand the gospel as urgent, relevant, and redemptive.

Ministerial Ethics and Attitudes

In his *Quarterly,* Moses Lard warned the young minister not "to play the dandy even by accident." For a spiritual leader such conduct is "utterly unallowable."[66] In a more negative tone, Alexander Campbell had declared in 1810 that the principles of the *Address* would "reduce hirelings, drones, idle shepherds, dumb dogs, blind guides and unfaithful watchmen to contempt."[67] Campbell, through the pages of the *Baptist* and *Harbinger,* acted the faithful watchman, throwing the light of his linguistics upon those bishops and evangelists lacking in morals and ethics. Messengers of God were to have a ministry of the spirit, by the spirit, and for the spirit. R. T. Matthews, dean of College of the Bible, Drake University, in 1894, believed "our reformation fathers" made an "excellent generalization" when they repeatedly taught that "God sends the Spirit, the Spirit fills the Apostles."[68] The spiritual preacher preaches what he experimentally knows of God's grace.

Discipline for infraction of ethics has been a difficult practical matter. Professor Millard, writing for the Connexion, said, "Once a year in conference, the character and standing of each minister is examined, that purity in the ministry may be carefully maintained."[69] The Stone Christians seemed better able to cope with this problem than the Reformers. Perhaps their sense of a professional ministry and the influences of the conference supplied the difference, the cohesiveness necessary for such control. C. C. Ware observes that in certain states the Disciples had conference control over the ethical conduct of the ministers. The North Carolina Constitution of the Christian Churches included:

Conference was to have discretionary power over the ministerial roll to be exercised advisedly and strictly each year and each church was to abide by the Conference decision to retain standing.[70]

Both Stone and Thomas Campbell contended that a selfish and domineering spirit among the clergy perpetuated disunity in the churches.[71] Thomas Campbell talked of "unsanctified professors" of Christianity and "unfaithful stewards" which the "proposed reformation would necessarily exclude."[72] The carrying out of this principle by the eldership in the Brush Run church is questionable. Remembering his own difficulty with the Presbytery, Thomas was most careful in harsh disciplinary action. Discipline in the Disciples has not evidenced any uniformity in principle or procedure. Under the heading of "Irresponsible Preachers" Alexander Campbell discussed, in the 1834 *Harbinger,* the situation of an Ohio preacher charged with "lasciviousness." Campbell held that God and the congregation could forgive him, but the local church "cannot restore the forgiven to any conspicuity in the congregation."[73]

William Robinson has aptly pointed out: "It is one thing for *Paul* to speak of 'coming with a rod,' but it is quite another thing—and a dangerous thing—for lesser men than Paul to follow his example."[74] Lesser men, often unaware of the larger spiritual content of Paul's theology, have crystalized thought and action patterns and sought to censure those outside the pale. It has often been an easy step from considering somene's theology suspect to suspecting his ethics and morals.

In Vol. 1, No. 1 of *The Evangelist* (1832), Walter Scott was questioned whether a church should issue a resolution against an elder who was believed guilty of unscriptural teaching. Too much of this has appeared in the periodicals of the movement. High points of such castigation preceded the

1906 formal separation between the Disciples of Christ and the churches of Christ and the division in the 1950's between the Disciples of Christ and the Christian churches. Attitudes have been a major concern in every generation. One area of conflict has been the attempt to bifurcate education and the Spirit. As in all denominations, the Disciples have had some ministers who have evidenced more education than wisdom. This group cannot distinguish the classroom from the pulpit. Walter Scott retorted, "The jangling of Philosophists and Philosophers cannot well be said to be less discordant and tiresome to the ear than that of theologues and theologians."[75] In an ironic article in 1907 C. A. Freer identified these souls as the "up-in-the-air class" who "like some rifles, are great repeaters." Though they may point with pride to "many degrees," they "seldom disturb the baptismal waters."[76] Elements in the movement still are not enamored with a sophisticated pulpit. An article in the 1967 *Gospel Advocate* complained of "too many intellectuals in the pew who are offended at the simplicity of the gospel, and too many scholars in the pulpit who put themselves in front of the cross."

Certain practices seem to concern the brotherhood periodically. One is the inability of a minister to "cut the strings" when he moves to another congregation. During the 1936 International Convention a resolution was presented, but tabled, urging the convention to "discourage the practice of ministers returning habitually to former fields for funerals and other occasions." This was deemed "both unethical and definitely harmful" to the present local pastor.[77] Other practices complained of in meetings and journals include the return to former pastorates for extended visits with leadership; criticizing the present pastor's program by comparison with the former procedures; failure to bolster the present pastor when complaints are communicated. Perhaps this whole area of ethical conduct is predicated upon spiritual and psychological immaturity and insecurity.

In the nineteenth century very little was written in the field of ministerial ethics. In 1941 the Home and State Missions Planning Council of the Disciples of Christ launched a study. In 1945 "My Ministerial Code of Ethics" came out of this research; and in 1949 Charles B. Tupper published *Called—in Honor.* The "Code" was a one-page certificate, two color, pertaining to personal conduct, church relationship to other ministers, the community, "My Communion," and the church universal. The book devoted a chapter to each of these subjects. For twenty years Disciples of Christ ministers were encouraged to sign the "Code" and hang it in the study as a "constant reminder" of the demands of the "high calling of the ministry." The section on "My Relationship to Fellow Ministers" reveals the problems of a century: "refuse to enter into unfair competition," "seek to serve my fellow ministers," "refrain from speaking disparagingly," "refrain from frequent visits to a former field," "never embarrass my successor by meddling," "not gossip about other ministers."

In "free churches" as the churches of Christ and Christian churches there must ever be an alertness by the ministry to arrogance, producing isolation, producing anarchy. No pastor is a law unto himself, and the very term brotherhood requires a mutuality of responsibility. When a man is ordained or recognized as a minister there is also laid upon his shoulders the ethical banner of the brotherhood. Two words become two works—humility and service. Each man serves his congregation and his brotherhood simultaneously. His badge of authority is Christ in his heart and His love on his hands.

In 1883 in *The Christian Minister's Manual,* F. M. Green published what he believed was the pastor's role:

> A Father's tenderness, a Shepherd's care,
> A Leader's courage, which the cross can bear,
> A Ruler's awe, a Watchman's wakeful eye,
> A Pilot's skill the helm in storms to ply;
> A Fisher's patience, and a Laborer's toil,
> A Guide's dexterity to disembroil,
> A Prophet's inspiration from above,
> A Teacher's Knowledge, and a Savior's love.

Notes to Chapter 8

1. C. C. Ware, *Barton Warren Stone* (St. Louis: Bethany Press, 1932), p. 334.

2. J. I. Rogers, *op. cit.,* cf. p. 147.

3. T. W. Grafton, *Alexander Campbell* (St. Louis: Christian Publishing Co. 1897), p. 182.

4. R. Richardson, *Memoirs of Alexander Campbell,* Vol. II (1898; reprint, Cincinnati: Standard Publishing), p. 582.

5. Archibald McLean, *Alexander Campbell as a Preacher: A Study* (St. Louis: Christian Publishing Co., 1908), p. 33.

6. *Millennial Harbinger* (January, 1842), p. 5.

7. *Christian Baptist,* Vol. VI (October, 1828), reprint, p. 58.

8. Thomas Munnell, *The Care of All the Churches,* p. 198.

9. Noel L. Keith, *The Story of D. S. Burnet: Undeserved Obscurity* (St. Louis: Bethany Press, 1954), p. 234.

10. D. L. Stevenson, *Walter Scott: Voice of the Golden Oracle,* p. 128.

11. J. J. Haley, *Makers and Molders of the Reformation Movement* (1914, reprint ed., Restoration Reprint Library, College Press), pp. 161, 162.

12. *The Evangelist,* Vol. I, No. 11 (November 5, 1832), reprint, p. 243.

13. W. T. Moore, *The New Living Pulpit of the Christian Church,* p. 30.

14. J. J. Haley, *Makers and Molders of the Reformation Movement,* p. 57.

15. *Ibid.*

16. *Millennial Harbinger* (1853), p. 546.

17. William J. Moore, *The New Testament Concept of the Ministry* (St. Louis: Bethany Press, 1956), p. 69.

18. *Millennial Harbinger* (Vol. IV, 1833), p. 373.

19. R. Richardson, *Memoirs of Alexander Campbell,* Vol. II, p. 599.

20. *Ibid.*

21. Robert Milligan, *Scheme of Redemption,* cf. pp. 364, 365.

22. *Lard's Quarterly* (April, 1865), p. 334.

23. *Christian Standard* (October 4, 1941), p. 1036.

24. J. A. Williams, *Life of Elder John Smith* (1870, reprint, Standard Publishing, 1904), cf. p. 180.

25. *Christian Baptist*, Vol. VII, p. 1829.

26. R. Richardson, *Memoirs of Alexander Campbell*, Vol. I, cf., p. 398.

27. J. A. Williams, *Life of Elder John Smith*, p. 181.

28. W. T. Moore, *The New Living Pulpit of the Christian Church*, p. 44.

29. *Lard's Quarterly*, Vol. I (September, 1863), (reprint ed., Rosemead, California: The Old Paths Book Club), p. 25.

30. *Abilene Christian College Bible Lectures, 1944* (Austin, Texas: Firm Foundation Publ. House, 1945), p. 134.

31. *Christian Standard* (October 11, 1970), p. 7.

32. J. M. Mathes, *Works of Elder B. W. Stone*, p. 324.

33. *Millennial Harbinger* (1840), p. 521.

34. *Millennial Harbinger* (1857), p. 415.

35. "Biblical Criticism," *Christian Standard* (February 3, 1906), p. 166.

36. *Women in the Church*, College of the Bible Quarterly (January, 1954), p. 12.

37. *Ibid.*

38. W. T. Moore, *Preacher Problems*, cf. p. 283.

39. "Shall the Sisters Speak?" *Women In the Church*, The College of the Bible Quarterly (January, 1954), cf. pp. 11-13.

40. *The Apostolic Guide* (May 14, 1886), n.p.

41. J. F. Burnet, *Early Women of the Christian Church* (Dayton, Ohio: Christian Publishing Assoc., 1921), p. 26.

42. Earl T. Sechler, *Sadie McCoy Crank* (Hermitage, Missouri: The Index, 1950), p. 14.

43. *The Christian* (September 23, 1973), p. 27.

44. Samuel F. Pugh, *Women's Place in the Total Church* (Indianapolis: United Christian Missionary Society, 1957), n.p.

45. *Ibid.*, cf. p. 9.

46. *Women in the Church, op. cit.*, p. 27.

47. "An Address on Female Education," *The Evangelist* (November, 1859), p. 484.

48. *The Christian* (October 7, 1973), p. 32.

49. *The Lookout* (October 24, 1971), p. 6.

50. W. R. Walker, *A Ministering Ministry* (Cincinnati: Standard Publishing, 1938), p. 161.

51. *Christian Standard* (March 21, 1971), p. 15.

52. Miriam Y. Holden, "The Role of Women in the Early Christian Church," *The Women's Pulpit* (April—June, 1955), p. 1.

53. Rufus Jones, "The Quakers," *Religious History of New England* (Cambridge: Harvard Univ. Press, 1917), p. 183.

54. "A Layman Talks to His Minister," *With Courage and Confidence* (Lexington: College of the Bible, 1957), p. 46.

55. Carroll C. Cotten, *The Imperative is Leadership,* p. 30.

56. *Stress in the Ministry* (Washington, D. C.: Ministry Studies Board, 1971).

57. Otis L. Castleberry, *They Heard Him Gladly* (Old Paths Publishing Co., 1963), p. 74.

58. Dwight E. Stevenson, *Disciples Preaching in the First Generation* (Nashville: Disciples of Christ Historical Society, 1969), p. 11.

59. *The Autobiography of J. W. McGarvey* (reprint, Lexington: College of the Bible, 1960), p. 49.

60. *Ibid.,* p. 66.

61. *Gospel Advocate* (January 26, 1967), p. 52.

62. *Christian Standard* (June 6, 1953), p. 357.

63. Perry Gresham, *Disciplines of the High Calling* (St. Louis: Bethany Press, 1954), p. 44.

64. James D. Murch, *Christian Minister's Manual* (Cincinnati: Standard Publishing, 1937), p. 16.

65. *The Christian-Evangelist* (October 7, 1953), p. 962.

66. *Lard's Quarterly* (April, 1865), cf. pp. 329-331.

67. R. Richardson, *Memoirs of Alexander Campbell,* Vol. I, p. 343.

68. *The New Christian Quarterly* (July, 1893), p. 259.

69. J. Winebrenner, *op. cit.*, p. 169.

70. Charles C. Ware, *North Carolina Disciples of Christ* (Christian Board of Publication, 1927), p. 126.

71. *Christian Messenger* (May, 1843), cf. pp. 33-38. Also *Declaration and Address*, pp. 13, 37.

72. *Declaration and Address*, p. 52.

73. *Millennial Harbinger* (December, 1834), p. 616.

74. *Adventuring For Christian Unity*, "Forward," p. 6.

75. *The Evangelist* (January 2, 1832), p. 22.

76. *The Christian-Evangelist* (January, 1907), p. 9.

77. *International Convention Addresses and Reports, 1936*, p. 354.